Goldendoodles

The Owners Guide from Puppy to Old Age

Choosing, Caring for, Grooming, Health, Training and Understanding Your Goldendoodle Dog

By Alan Kenworthy

Copyright and Trademarks

Disclaimer and Legal Notice

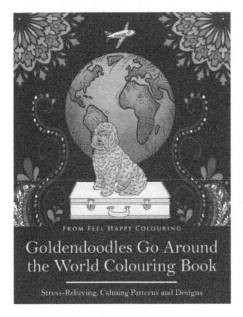

FROM FEEL HAPPY COLOURING

Goldendoodles Go Around
the World Colouring Book

Stress-Relieving, Calming Patterns and Designs

Foreword

Once you've read this book, you will have all the information you need to make a well-informed decision about whether or not the Goldendoodle is the breed for you, and you will know how to care for them at every stage of their life.

As an owner, expert trainer and professional dog whisperer, I would like to teach you the human side of the equation, so you can learn how to think more like your dog and eliminate behavioral problems with your pet.

If you're someone like me, who encounters many dogs in their daily life, you may suddenly be hearing the word "doodle" a lot. This is shorthand for various hybrid or "designer" dogs that have a Poodle for a parent.

My first experience with a "doodle" was a Labradoodle, a breed originally cultivated as a low-allergy guide dog. The mix proved so successful in the eyes of almost everyone who encountered the dogs that other Poodle mixes began being developed.

The second "doodle" to gain notoriety was the Cockapoo, a cross between a Cocker Spaniel and Poodle. Then the Goldendoodle (or Goldypoo) entered the mix out of a desire for a slightly larger "doodle" cross.

Goldendoodles live up to the hybrid expectation. They tend to exhibit extremely balanced personalities and high intelligence. I think they are fantastic family dogs and certainly a breed that gets on well with children.

I can't say enough good things about the Goldendoodle, and can heartily recommend him as a near-perfect canine friend.

Acknowledgments

In writing this book, I also sought tips, advice, photos and opinions from 32 experts of the Goldendoodle dog breed.

In particular I wish to thank the following wonderful experts for going out of their way to help and contribute:

USA & CANADA

Amy Lane of Fox Creek Farm Goldendoodles
http://www.goldendoodles.net/

April Cliber of Cliberdoodle
http://www.cliberdoodle.com/

Janet Wright of Okefeild Acres
http://www.okefeildacres.com/

Lynne Porter-Whitmire of Fountain Falls Goldendoodles
http://www.ffgoldendoodles.com

Nathan Crockett of Best Goldendoodles
http://bestgoldendoodles.com/

Renee Sigman of Yesteryear Acres
http://www.yesteryearacres.com

Janece Schommer of Goldendoodle Acres
http://www.goldendoodleacres.com/

Bev and Arnie Eckert of Hilltop Pups LLC
http://hilltoppups.net/

Acknowledgments

Wendi Loustau of The Mustard Seed Ranch
http://www.mustardseeddoodles.com/

Donna Schlosser of Suwanee Goldendoodles
http://www.suwaneegoldendoodles.com

Beth Engelbert of Lakeview Doodles
http://www.lakeviewdoodles.com

Carol McDonald of Rainbows End Puppies
http://rainbowsendpuppies.com/

Melissa Farmer of Farmer Doodles
http://www.farmerdoodles.com/

Candice Farrell of Ooodles of Doodles
http://ooodlesofdoodles.com/

Judith Peabody of MorningShine MountainDoods
http://www.doodlesofvermont.com/

Bobbie Yoder of Little Mountain Doodles
http://www.littlemountaindoodles.4t.com/

Bart Hainz of Heartland Goldens and Mini Goldendoodles
http://www.heartlandgoldensanddoodles.com/

Sharon Ruff of Ruff'n Ready Doodles
http://www.ruffnreadydoodles.ca/

Christy Stevens of Winding Creek Ranch Goldendoodles
http://www.thewindingcreekranch.com

Cherrie Mahon of River Valley Doodles
http://www.rivervalleydoodles.com/

Laura Chaffin of Cimarron Frontier Doodles
http://www.cimarronfrontierdoodles.4t.com/

Tara Mitchell of Apple Creek Doodles
http://www.applecreekdoodles.com

UNITED KINGDOM

Donna Shaw of Donakell Goldendoodles
http://www.donakellgoldendoodles.co.uk

Photo Credit: Stephanie Mahley Photography and Lynne Porter-Whitmire of Fountain Falls Goldendoodles

Table of Contents

Table of Contents

Table of Contents

Table of Contents

Table of Contents

Table of Contents

Chapter 1 – Meet the Goldendoodle

Among the many hybrid dogs available, the "Goldendoodle" is a favorite for its well-balanced personality. Friendly, gentle, affectionate and smart, the breed rarely shows aggression. A Goldendoodle (sometimes called a Goldypoo in the UK) is a superb family pet and one of the most successful of all hybrid crosses.

The mix starts with crossing a Golden Retriever and a Poodle. Deeper generations involve crossing Goldendoodles back to either parent breed or breeding two Goldendoodles together.

Not all Goldendoodles look the same. There are three coat types – wavy, curly and flat. The wavy and curly coats will continue to grow and will need periodic visits to the groomer, typically every 8 weeks. These coat types will need to be brushed regularly to prevent matting. The flat coats typically shed and do not need trims or daily brushing.

Goldendoodles have a reputation as an excellent "first time" dog. They respond well to training, which is a must. Goldendoodles are so "high" on life, they can bowl over children and smaller adults with an exuberant greeting.

Beyond that, however, they are easy to care for and delightfully people oriented. A Goldendoodle has one thought in mind when he comes into your life: "Hi! Let's be best friends!"

They crave the company of people and excel as therapy and service dogs. The breed has an unusual capacity for intuition and can read human emotion with uncanny accuracy. While an excellent trait in a companion dog, a Goldendoodle does not like to be left alone for long periods of time. Some dogs can develop separation anxiety that may manifest with destructive chewing and digging, although proper training can prevent this.

A Goldendoodle needs at least 30 minutes of daily exercise and makes an excellent jogging or swimming buddy. They love water and will dive right in a pool or lake, or just chase the sprinkler in the front yard.

Playful by nature, these dogs like to hear their owners laugh and will invent games to get you involved in the fun.

Goldendoodles always seem to be smiling! They'll play fetch until they drop and are naturals at agility sports. The more intellectually challenging the task, the better.

The breed is typically healthy but can be subject to any disease or condition present in either Golden Retrievers or Poodles. We discuss this more in our chapter on health.

Goldendoodle Breed History and Genetics

Goldendoodles were developed in the 1990s in North America and Australia, building off the wild success of the Labradoodle and Cockapoo mixes. The goal was to achieve a slightly larger "doodle" with the desired traits of minimal shedding and low dander production, making them better tolerated by allergy sufferers than other breeds.

Since the breed is still relatively "new," it is quite common for available puppies to be first generation (F1) crosses between a Golden Retriever and a Standard Poodle. The typical mature weight is 50-75 lbs.

When an F1 Goldendoodle is bred back to a Standard Poodle, their puppies are known as F1b dogs. F1b dogs are likely to have a fuller, curlier coat with about a 90% chance of being non-shedding.

If an F1 Goldendoodle is bred to another F1, the puppies would be classified as F2s.

The multigen Goldendoodle (short for multigeneration) is the product of breeding two Goldendoodle parents that are at least second generation crosses. They were first bred in 2006.

Now, multigens are quite commonplace with breeders who have moved on to higher generations, breeding into the 4th generation. Breeders have to spend time developing their lines to the multigen level, so unless a new breeder buys Goldendoodle breeding stock from another breeder, they have to start with a Golden Retriever and Poodle. The multigen Goldendoodle is gaining popularity as more breeders are breeding deeper generations, however, early generation Goldendoodles (F1s or F1bs) still remain popular with many owners, as well as breeders.

Most wavy and curly multigens do not shed, where flat-coated Goldendoodles will almost definitely have some degree of mild shedding. The increased success of non-shedding coats in the F1bs and multigens is the primary reason for the growing popularity of the deeper generations of Goldendoodles.

Given the Goldendoodle is a cross of the Golden Retriever and the Poodle, some insight into the foundation breeds is helpful to understand what you are getting.

Golden Retrievers

The Golden Retriever is a popular and much-beloved dog, prized for his gentle, intelligent nature and unwavering loyalty. A Golden is one of the most reliable of all canines. They are friendly even with strangers and fantastic family dogs, exhibiting supreme patience and protectiveness with children. They love attention and are playful and fun companions.

The coat ranges from blonde to a deep red and is considered somewhat long. The breed stands 21-24 inches (53.34-60.96 cm) and weighs 60-85 lbs. / 27.2-38.5 kg.

Standard Poodle

The Standard Poodle is an active, intelligent dog. They do not shed and are excellent family companions, although given to territoriality and a strong protective streak.

They are very good with children and are excellent watchdogs. Nothing goes on in a Poodle's world that he doesn't notice and evaluate.

A Standard Poodle stands 15-27 inches (38.1-68.58 cm) and weighs 45-70 lbs. / 20.5-32 kg. They are long-legged, lean dogs that come in a variety of colors.

Photo Credit: Rosie from April Cliber of Cliberdoodle

But Wait! There's More!

So far I've only discussed Goldendoodles with a Standard Poodle parent, but there are also Toy and Mini Poodles, and the European Golden Retriever. When these possibilities are thrown into the "Doodle" mix, the classification of the Goldendoodle gets much more complex.

Size is often used to draw the distinction:

Petite range: Height below 14 inches, typically 25 lbs. or less (11.36kg).

Miniature range: Height over 14 but under 17 inches (35cm to 42cm) at the withers, typically 26-35 lbs. (11.82-15.91kg).

Medium range: Height over 17 but under 21 inches (43cm to 52cm) at the withers, typically 36-50 lbs. (16.36-22.73kg).

Standard range: Height over 21 inches (53cm to 63cm) at the withers, typically 51 or more lbs. (23.18kg).

The European Golden Retriever is used to breed the English Cream Goldendoodle (sometimes called the "Teddy Bear" Goldendoodle). These dogs are stockier with square heads, a broad muzzle and shorter legs. They tend to be solid and less lanky than their American counterparts. The coat also is denser and thicker.

Physical Characteristics of the Goldendoodle

Clearly in describing the physical characteristics of the Goldendoodle, the range of attributes is broad:

* **Height:** 12-32 inches / 30.48-81.28 cm at the withers.
* **Weight:** 9-150 lbs. / 4-68 kg
* **Colors:** Cream/Blonde, Golden, Apricot, Red, Chocolate, Silver, Black, White

There are also frosted, phantom and tricolor coat variations. Most Goldendoodles have brown eyes, but green, blue, amber and multi-colors are also possible.

The coat will be shaggy (wavy), curly or smooth (flat) depending on the genetic mix of the individual.

Amy Lane of Fox Creek Farm gives us an insight into the probability of coat types:

"I find the same variety in a multigen litter as you would find in an F1 or F1b litter. Some dogs carry for curl and some dogs don't. We can now test for this. It is a recessive gene.

Therefore, if both parents carry for curl, the entire litter will be curly. If one parent carries for curl and one doesn't, you will have a mixed litter of wavy and curly puppies.

If both parents do not carry for curl, you will have all wavy puppies. This is the same for the flat coat. The gene is called the IC (incorrect coat gene). Again, this gene is recessive meaning both parents have to be a carrier for some of the puppies to have the flat coat.

Since Poodles typically do not carry the IC gene and do carry for curl and the Golden Retriever is the opposite, F1 litters typically have a mix of wavy and curly coats and no flat coated puppies. Most F1s carry the IC gene and that is the reason breeding two F2s together gives flat coats. I have successfully avoided producing flat-coated puppies since this DNA marker has been discovered."

Hypoallergenic

Nathan Crockett of Best Goldendoodles has some useful clarifications on this much-misunderstood term: "A lot of confusion persists in the dog world about whether a particular breed is 'hypoallergenic.' Most people think the term hypoallergenic means non-allergenic. Hypoallergenic does NOT mean non-allergenic. The prefix 'hypo-' simply means 'below.' Someone suffering from hypothermia has a body temperature significantly below normal. So something that is hypoallergenic has a below average chance of causing allergies. In this sense, many low to non-shedding breeds of dogs are truly hypoallergenic, because they are less likely to cause allergies than other breeds of dogs. Since many Goldendoodles have low to no shedding (especially F1b crosses and even more so the multigens), they can be called hypoallergenic.

Additionally, not all allergies are caused by shedding hair. The vast majority of dog allergies are due to reactions to dog hair or dog hair dander, but occasionally people are allergic to dog saliva (which obviously can't be solved by getting a non-shedding dog)."

Photo Credit: April Cliber of Cliberdoodle

Service Dogs

A service dog is a type of assistance dog specifically trained to help people who have disabilities, including visual difficulties, hearing impairments, mental illness, seizures, diabetes, autism and more. Goldendoodles are excelling in this role. Amy Lane of Fox Creek Farm tells us her personal experiences:

"In 2003, I donated an F1 standard male Goldendoodle puppy to Guide Dogs of America in Los Angeles, CA. I felt that the Goldendoodle had the necessary qualities to excel in service work. The puppy was appropriately named 'Richter' as his coat was described as being similar to the Richter scale. As with most service dogs, Richter was cared for and trained by a puppy raiser for 18 months and then turned over to the organization for more formalized training. He achieved his certification as the first Goldendoodle seeing eye dog on 5/1/05.

Since then, Goldendoodles have been donated by many breeders and trained as seeing eye dogs, service dogs, hearing dogs, diabetic alert dogs and PTSD dogs. They have participated in reading programs in schools and perhaps where they have excelled the most is as therapy dogs that visit nursing homes and hospitals."

Goldendoodle Dog Breed Standard

As a hybrid or "designer" dog, there is no set breed standard for the Goldendoodle as would be seen in a recognized breed. The Goldendoodle Association of North America (GANA) determined at its inception that a breed standard would not be developed until the multigen Goldendoodle was commonplace and ideal standards could be determined.

They state "[t]he items below represent the items determined to be important in the development of the Goldendoodle and our member breeders have voted upon and agreed that these will be the basis for which the rest of the breed standard is created."

- A balanced mix of physical characteristics of the Golden Retriever and the Poodle;

- A consistently friendly, social temperament similar to that of the Golden Retriever;

- Consists of Poodle and Golden Retriever only – no other breed infusion is accepted;

- No tail docking or body altering other than the removal of dew claws – dew claw removal is optional.

The Goldendoodle Puppy

Having a new puppy in the house can mean dealing with the aftermath of a little dog's big ideas. The babies are so cute, though, it's hard to stay mad at them long. In the midst of all the fun, however, there are major responsibilities to face. Puppies take work!

A dog's adult temperament and behavior are largely shaped during the first few weeks in a new home. As a pet owner, you hope to have a happy companion that is obedient and well mannered. Goldendoodles can be overly exuberant, but they respond superbly to training, which is to your advantage.

You have a long "to do" list of goals with your new friend:

- puppy proofing the house before the dog's arrival

- crate and house training
- establishing a healthy diet
- setting a grooming routine
- begin a program of socialization

This is the time to get ahead of undesirable behaviors like jumping, whining and barking. It's important to ask yourself — and to be honest — about the amount of time you have to spend with your Goldendoodle. That's a question not just for today, but for as much as 15 or 16 years down the road.

If your work, school and social schedules are so active your dog will be sitting at home alone most of the time, be responsible and don't adopt a dog of any kind!

Goldendoodles love their humans and want to be with them. Do not make a selfish decision about adoption. Think about the long-term welfare of the Goldendoodle!

The Need for Socialization

Any breed can develop bad habits and become an obnoxious nuisance. Plan on starting training with your Goldendoodle by 10-12 weeks of age. (Most vets recommend that the dog finish the required rabies, distemper and parvovirus vaccinations before being taken to a class with other animals.)

When you send your dog to school, you are there as a student as well. The Goldendoodle isn't the only one who needs to learn a few lessons. Your role is to be "leader of the pack" and stop your very intelligent pet from getting away with bloody murder. Trust me, a compliant human can be putty in the paws of a Goldendoodle!

If you don't know how to be the "alpha," you need to get to

class and learn quickly, for your sake and for that of your dog!

One or Two?

When you are sitting on the floor surrounded by puppies, adopting two seems like the best idea in the world. You might want to pause and take a breath. Adopting a single dog is a big commitment. You are pledging your time and money to a living creature. With the second dog, all of that doubles.

It is true that Goldendoodles will be happier with a companion, but these are people dogs. If you aren't careful, you'll just have two lonely, bored dogs on your hands, which means twice the destruction when they start thinking of ways to entertain and console themselves.

Goldendoodles are receptive to new additions to the family. Pace yourself. Start with one dog and see how it goes. There's nothing that says you have to adopt the second dog at the same time you take in the first.

With Other Pets

Goldendoodles get along well with other pets. The "person" most likely to object is the family cat. Don't try to play the role of United Nations in this relationship. Exercise a supervisory presence and reinforce good behavior with praise and treats, but don't over-react. Expect a lot of mouthy "trash talking" and paw swipes from the cat. Don't be surprised if the puppy is the one who needs protection. After all, your cat is fully "weaponized."

Don't force the animals to spend time together. When the puppy arrives, let the cat check out the new family member with the dog safely in his crate. There may not be a total peace agreement in the beginning, but a détente will work itself out.

Over time, Goldendoodles and cats tend to get along better as the two animals come to know one another. If it does become necessary to separate your pets, just be calm, use a firm "no" and let them try again later. The whole process may take several weeks, so be patient.

As for other types of pets, use reasonable caution. It would not, for instance, be a great idea to let any kind of dog play with a rabbit. As for creatures like birds or fish, dogs tend to just ignore them.

Male or Female?

Gender truly is not an issue in determining personality. The decision only becomes critical if you are considering breeding your dog. Focus on personality and heredity by making a good choice from a reputable breeder. A dog's genetics and his life experiences matter much more in his eventual temperament and behavior.

Many people make the mistake of assuming female dogs have a better nature and are sweeter. There is no basis for this assumption. If a female dog has been spoiled and coddled as a puppy, she will exhibit more territoriality and even aggression as an adult than a male.

The number one reason most people cite for not wanting a male dog is urine marking and spraying. All good breeders require a spay/neuter contract to be signed at the time of purchase. If for some reason your Goldendoodle hasn't been spayed or neutered, have this done before six months of age for the health benefits of the procedure and to avoid unplanned litters.

The surgery brings down hormone levels in the dog's system. This will put an end to territorial urine marking in males and will save females the moodiness they often exhibit when they go into heat.

Beyond these considerations, both males and females make excellent family pets. The importance in choosing gender is only really important when there is an existing dog at home where pairing for compatibility is the goal. Each puppy is born with their own temperament and degree of dominance. Spaying/neutering before six months typically keeps that inborn dominance to a minimum because the hormones have been removed.

The key is this – if your existing (older) dog has territorial tendencies or believes that the entire house is his/her domain, then getting a pup with the opposite gender is usually regarded as best. Even so (although unlikely), you can still have a boy/girl combo that fight just as much as two girls or two boys. There will often be a struggle to determine who is alpha between the two.

Test your own dog out in public. If they get along great with either gender wherever they go, then they will get along with either gender at home. Most Goldendoodles are easy going and love the second furry addition.

With Children

Goldendoodles are terrific dogs for kids. This breed can get pretty rambunctious, however, and may easily knock smaller children down. Since excited jumping is a habit that you will want to curb in your dog, focus on training your puppy to have all four feet on the ground while greeting your family and friends.

The point is not to let your child develop a fear of dogs. Explain to your child the dog is just excited and happy. By nature, Goldendoodles are very gentle, loving and loyal. They just require a bit of training in the beginning to get a good start on their life as a family pet.

Be sure that your children understand the proper way to interact with all animals — kindly and with respect. Don't leave a young child alone with a dog, no matter how good-natured you believe the animal to be. If a child hurts the dog, perhaps by pulling its tail or ears, the dog may react instinctually. Don't put either in that position.

Photo Credit: Nathan Crockett of Best Goldendoodles

Puppy or Adult Dog?

There really is no need to explain why people love puppies so much. They are cute beyond words, and if you adopt a dog at a young age, your pet will be with you for up to 15-16 years.

If, however, you don't have your heart set on a puppy, adopting an adult from a shelter or a rescue situation is a tremendous act of kindness. I wholeheartedly support the lifesaving work of these organizations. There is an appalling epidemic of homeless companion animals in the world.

Find out why the animal has been given up for adoption. It may simply be a case of a dog that has been living with an elderly person whose human has died or gone into a nursing home. Goldendoodles can be too energetic for some people, but in a home where they can receive attention and get enough exercise, they are the perfect pets.

Even if you don't decide to adopt a dog under these circumstances, please consider supporting the work of rescue organizations with your donations or volunteer hours.

The International Doodle Owners Group is dedicated to Goldendoodle rescue, education and support:

http://idogrescue.com/

Famous Goldendoodles and Their Owners

The growing popularity of the Goldendoodle means these pets are now found in some rather famous households:

- Ellen DeGeneres
- Usher
- Ricky Lake
- Perez Hilton
- Ashley Tisdale
- Jamie Lee Curtis
- Frank and Kathy Lee Gifford
- Kenny Chesney
- Peter Krause
- Susan Feniger

Chapter 2 – Getting Serious About Adoption

At the point at which you are no longer just "thinking" about a Goldendoodle, but are interested in talking to breeders and really finding a puppy, you should go into a potential transaction armed with a few basics.

Photo Credit: Renee Sigman of Yesteryear Acres

Is a Goldendoodle Dog for You?

Answering the question, "Is a Goldendoodle right for me?" isn't as simple as answering the same question with the name of a purebred dog inserted. I am not, under any circumstances, talking down crossbred dogs or Goldendoodles in particular when I say you are taking a greater roll of the dice adopting a hybrid mix.

My late father was something of a dog whisperer. A great deal of what I know about successfully interacting with dogs, I learned from him. For most of his life, he had crossbreeds, or, to put a finer point on it, mutts. Daddy had an ability to pick good dogs that was, in my opinion, rather uncanny.

Late in life, however, as his mobility was severely compromised, he had a series of Yorkshire Terriers, a breed he chose for their small size and fiercely loyal disposition. He liked dogs that were confident to the point of being a little feisty, so he did well in choosing Yorkies.

All Goldendoodles are not the same. Under the very best of circumstances, the dog will exhibit all the sterling qualities of good disposition, intelligence and gentleness I've already described.

However, if you get a dog that is the product of a casual backyard pairing, or worse yet, one from a puppy mill, you might be getting an animal that is a genetic mess with little or no socialization and a myriad of potential health problems. Picking a good breeder is as important with a hybrid dog as with a purebred.

Going into the adoption, you need to ask yourself some serious questions based on the educated guesses you can make about what life with a Goldendoodle will be like.

- Are you in a place in your personal and professional life where you can devote time and attention to a dog that needs at least 30 minutes of exercise a day and bonds very deeply with his human?

- Will you commit to grooming your Goldendoodle's coat on a weekly basis as both an aspect of appearance and good health? And will you make the financial commitment to have the dog professionally groomed 3-4 times a year?

- Can you handle the fact that although you may have a picture of what you think a Goldendoodle looks like in your mind, the puppy you adopt may not grow up to fit that preconception? Can you accept the fact that not all Goldendoodles are the same?

If you are confident about moving forward with an adoption, you should know how to choose a puppy that presents with good health and at least the basic indications of a good temperament.

Finding and Picking a Puppy

Although finding a breeder for a crossbreed dog can often be difficult, this really isn't the case with Goldendoodles. They are very popular dogs and have become well established in both the United States and Europe.

The dogs in the United Kingdom and on the Continent are usually bred from European Golden Retrievers. They are heavier dogs with shorter legs and a somewhat boxier appearance, but they typically exhibit the same positive qualities we've been discussing for all Goldendoodles.

Learn Basic Health Evaluation Tips

Before you start gushing over the puppies you are shown, learn the following quick tips that will help you to pick a healthy puppy to take home.

- It is not unusual for a puppy to be sleepy at first. The dog should wake up quickly, however. You want to see puppies that are energetic, alert and just a little mischievous.

- When you handle the baby, it should feel well-nourished in your hands. Feel for just a little fat over the rib area, and look for dogs that have a plump, healthy appearance with well-developed roundness.

- The puppy's coat should look and feel healthy, with a good shine and no sign of bald patches, dandruff or greasiness.

- Watch the puppy walk and run. Although potentially a little wobbly, the dog should not have any obvious physical impairment like a limp or an abnormal gait.

- Select a puppy with bright, clear eyes. There should not be any sign of discharge or encrusted matter around the eyes or on the muzzle.

- Listen to the puppy breathe. Respiration should be steady and quiet with no sneezing or coughing. Check the nostrils for signs of discharge or crusty matter.

- Turn the dog over and examine the area around the anus and genitals. Make sure there is no visible collection of fecal matter or any areas filled with pus.

- When the puppy is looking away from you, test its hearing by clapping your hands. The dog should give a visible reaction that indicates it has registered the sound.

- Conduct a vision test by rolling a ball at the dog. Note how the puppy notices and reacts to the motion and the accuracy with which it interacts with the toy.

When you feel confident with the fundamentals of choosing a

healthy puppy, start working on your shortlist of breeders. Visiting websites is the way to find almost anything in our modern world, but, as we will discuss shortly, you will need to be aware of and avoid scams. I believe that it is imperative you find several breeders within driving distance of your home so that you can make at least one visit to the facility before adopting your pet.

Photo Credit: Amy Lane of Fox Creek Farm

Locating Breeders to Consider

A good place to begin your search in the United States is either the Goldendoodle Association of North America (GANA) or goldendoodles.com – both also have an extensive list of breeders on their websites:

http://www.goldendoodleassociation.com
http://www.goldendoodles.com

Consider contacting your local dog club or speaking with your vet about recommendations. Looking for advertisements in local newspapers and magazines is a dicey proposition. The dogs you will see listed there will most likely be puppies for sale through "backyard breeders."

In many cases, such a breeder is a perfectly well-intentioned, legitimate soul who has allowed their pet to breed. That is not an inherently "wrong" situation, but such people will be able to tell you very little about the genetics of the animals involved. When you adopt a puppy through this kind of arrangement, I strongly urge seeking an evaluation from a veterinarian before agreeing to take the dog.

More disturbingly, however, the classified ads are the prime stalking grounds of puppy mills, deplorable operations that exist only to produce dogs in bulk for profit. Never adopt a dog from any circumstance where you are not allowed to meet the parents and siblings.

You should be able to see for yourself where the puppy was born and evaluate how it has been living for the first few weeks of its life. Even if you are dealing with a breeder online at some distance, modern technology should allow you to see the entire litter via videoconference and take a remote tour of the facilities before visiting in person.

Seeing the parents, verifying their health and discussing the dogs with a knowledgeable breeder are fundamental to a successful adoption. If you are working with a responsible owner who is enthusiastic about the Goldendoodle breed, they will be more than willing to give you all this information and more!

Listen to your gut. If you are uncomfortable with the person with whom you are dealing or think there is something wrong with the adoption, move on! (And if you feel that the dogs you have been shown are being exploited or mistreated in any way, report the operation to animal welfare.)

The Timing of Your Adoption Matters

In adopting a dog from a breeder, timing is important. If any facility tells you that they have puppies available at all times, that is a red flag that you are dealing with a puppy mill, as domesticated dogs only come into heat approximately every 6 months. Therefore, responsible breeders will only breed twice a year.

It is much more normal for a prospective adoptive "parent" to be placed on a waiting list. (Don't be surprised if you are asked to put down a small deposit to reserve a dog from an impending litter. Typically, if you opt not to take one of the dogs, the amount is refunded to you. Don't assume this, however. Find out the terms of the transaction in advance.)

Also consider the timing of your own life in contemplating an adoption. If you are in the middle of a big project at work, or it's one of the hectic holiday times of the year, it's probably not a great idea to bring a puppy into the chaos.

Dogs, especially highly intelligent ones like Goldendoodles, respond best to routine. You want to give the puppy a secure start as your companion. This means time to bond and time for the little dog to learn the ropes of how your household runs during normal everyday life.

Approximate Purchase Price

It is often difficult to give a price range for a hybrid mix like a

Goldendoodle because puppies can be born under such widely varying circumstances. If, for instance, you are looking at classified ads, you may see puppies listed for as little as $50 / £31. Do not treat this adoption as a bargain hunt. When you purchase a dog under those circumstances, there are no guarantees about health, disposition or genetic quality.

The best way to ensure you are getting the best Goldendoodle possible is to work with a breeder that supports an organized breeding program with set goals for desirable traits. That means you'll be paying as much as $2500 / £1600 (or more), but the higher price will be well worth it. Think of it this way: given a projected lifespan of roughly 14 years, that works out to about $178 / £118 a year.

These websites can be good places to begin your search:

Adopt a Pet — http://www.adoptapet.com
Petango — http://www.petango.com
Pet Finder — http://www.petfinder.com
GANA - http://www.goldendoodleassociation.com
GoldenDoodles.com - http://goldendoodles.com/

Pros and Cons of Owning a Goldendoodle

I'm always drawn up short by the idea of discussing the pros and cons of a breed as if it's a cut-and-dried matter. What one person adores in a dog, another might not be able to tolerate. I have a friend who raises Jack Russell Terriers. They are incredibly smart dogs, and I wouldn't have one for anything in the world. Talk about alpha! Jack Russells might as well be four-legged drill sergeants, but to my friend, they are the perfect companions. I like laid-back breeds that see the allure of the couch as much as the pull of a forced march. Goldendoodles fit that bill nicely.

When you find a breeder who really loves Goldendoodles, that person should be ready and willing to discuss both the positives and negatives of the breed. They do so out of one prevailing goal – to see these exceptional animals go to the best homes possible.

Photo Credit: Renee Sigman of Yesteryear Acres

Reasons to Adopt a Goldendoodle

- Many are better tolerated by allergy sufferers
- Excellent dogs for active families
- Respond well to training
- Known to have a good disposition
- Long lifespan and overall good health

Reasons NOT to adopt a Goldendoodle

- Not a recognized and standardized breed
- No guarantees of low allergy reaction
- Many puppies can tend to get overly excited
- Heavily targeted for "puppy mill" breeding

Chapter 3 – Buying a Goldendoodle

In pedigreed adoptions, puppies are classified as "pet" or "show" quality, with prices set accordingly. While you won't run into this distinction with a hybrid dog like a Goldendoodle, a reputable breeder won't just sell to anyone who walks through the door with the asking price.

Expect many of the same requirements seen in pedigreed adoption agreements. For instance, you may be asked to comply with spaying or neutering the dog before it reaches six months of age. Many puppies will already have been spayed or neutered by the breeder. There should also be some genetic information supplied to you, along with all existing medical records and a standard health guarantee.

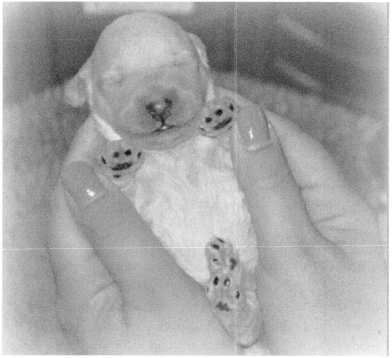

Photo Credit: April Cliber of Cliberdoodle

When you work with a "backyard" breeder, these terms won't apply. This doesn't mean you're getting an inferior dog, just that your risk is greater in important areas like genetic quality, health and future behavior.

How to Choose a Breeder

I strongly advocate working with a local breeder or one at a reasonable traveling distance rather than agreeing to have your puppy shipped to you. There is simply too much that can and does go wrong subjecting a young animal to the hazards of travel.

Additionally, if you find your Goldendoodle online, I believe visiting the breeder at least once is imperative. If at all possible, you should always pick up your dog in person.

If a breeder is unwilling to have you visit their facility, be suspicious. The same goes for breeders that are only willing to let you see one puppy. Always ask to meet both parents if possible and to see the entire litter.

You need to see for yourself how the dogs are living and the level of care they have received. When you work with a breeder, the sense should be that information is flowing freely back and forth between you. The breeder should openly discuss the good and bad things about the Goldendoodle cross.

April Cliber of Cliberdoodle explains the home guardian concept, which is becoming increasingly commonplace: "Nowadays many breeders are now home based and their dogs live in the house as pets. Puppies are typically raised in the breeder's home as well. It's very common for Goldendoodle breeders to use guardian homes for their breeding dogs. A guardian home is a permanent family for the dog. The breeder retains ownership of the dog during the years the dog is used for breeding, however, the dog lives with the guardian family. This arrangement is great for the dog because once retired from breeding, he/she is spayed/neutered and returned to its forever family. There is no need to re-home the dog after its breeding career has ended. There are still breeders who use kennels, but the numbers of home breeders is quite high."

What to Expect from a Good Breeder

Breeders are concerned about the dog's long-term welfare and will help you pick your puppy. In the process, expect to be asked questions about your life, especially your schedule, family and other pets. Please don't be offended. You are working with a breeder because you want access to Goldendoodle experts. Having someone who understands these dogs and can evaluate the correctness of the placement is to the benefit of all involved. If a breeder doesn't show this kind of interest, it's a reason for concern.

The Breeder Should Provide the Following

Even though the adoption process for your Goldendoodles may be less formal, the transaction should involve the following:

- *contract of sale* - This document explains the transfer of records and all paperwork, and details the responsibilities of both parties.

- *information packet* - This should be a collection of advice and recommendations for things like vaccinations, feeding, training and exercise.

- *description of ancestry* - This description should give the names and types of Golden Retriever and Poodle used in the mix and any other information about those dogs that might be of relevance.

- *health records* - At the same time that you take possession of the puppy, you should receive detailed records of all medical procedures, including vaccinations that have been performed. These records should also disclose any potential genetic issues.

- *health guarantee* - This guarantee affirms the health of the puppy at the time of adoption and may require confirmation of that fact by a vet within a set period of time.

Warning Signs of a Bad Breeder

Some of the signs that indicate you may be working with a bad breeder include the following:

- Assurances that there is no need for you to come to the breeder facilities in person.

- Being told that you can buy your puppy sight unseen with complete confidence.

- Being allowed to come to the kennel or home, but being denied permission to see where the dogs are currently living.

- Seeing any facility where dogs live in overcrowded conditions and seem to be apprehensive and nervous around people.

- Having no access to meet either of the puppies' parents or no verifiable information about them.

- Breeders who can't or won't produce health records on the dogs or who tell you that they will get the records and send them to you.

- Failure to provide a health guarantee and to discuss what will happen (including a refund) if the puppy gets sick.

- No signed bill of sale or vague promises that one will be sent to you.

Photo Credit: Judith Peabody of MorningShine MountainDoods

Avoiding Scam Puppy Sales

Puppy mills exist to make money only. The dogs receive little to no health care. They are usually housed in terrible conditions. Inbreeding is common, as are genetic abnormalities and health problems. The females suffer from carrying one litter after another — NO ONE wants to support these cruel, for-profit scams.

Some scammers will advertise a single puppy on the free-to-advertise websites and get you to pay a "deposit" over the Internet. They leave the advert open long enough to rake in a number of deposits, then remove the ad and create a new one from a different location.

Unfortunately, the Internet is full of these kinds of operations, as are many pet stores. If you don't have the money to work with a breeder, think about a shelter or rescue adoption. You will be helping an animal in need and saving a life.

Puppy mills capitalize on the growing popularity of crossbreed dogs like Goldendoodles. Remember, if the following requirements can't be met, you have reason to be suspicious:

- Pay a personal visit to the home or kennel where the puppies were born and where they are currently living.

- Meet both the parents and learn something about their background.

- Have a full tour of all areas where the dogs are kept.

- Receive medical records and all health information, including anything related to genetics.

Best Age to Purchase a Puppy

A Goldendoodle puppy needs time to learn important life skills from the mother dog, including eating solid food and grooming themselves.

For the first month of a puppy's life, they will be on a mother's milk-only diet. Once the puppy's teeth begin to appear, they will start to be weaned from mother's milk, and by the age of 8 weeks should be completely weaned and eating just puppy food.

Puppies generally leave between 7-9 weeks and are usually weaned before they receive their first vaccines. It is not beneficial for the pup to stay longer, as it can have a negative effect. In some cases, the mom is too overwhelmed with the size of the pups and the size of the litter and she avoids them. This occurs as early as 6 weeks old and can result in bad behaviors as the puppies interact with each other. Their roughhouse playing becomes more and more imprinted on them, and families could struggle to teach the puppy not to play with children as they do with their litter mates.

Trainers would even highly recommend training and bonding begin with their new families by 8-10 weeks. In addition, pups need to be highly socialized between 8-12 weeks with new people, new experiences and new places. This time period is very crucial in developing a well-rounded pup.

With vet approval being required in some states, a breeder can place pups a little earlier than 8 weeks if the puppies show signs of being properly weaned and being socially mature enough. In fact, every mommy/litter experience will be a little different. It's up to the breeder to evaluate each litter individually and determine the best timing for release based primarily on proper weaning and maturity.

Amy Lane of Fox Creek Farm gives us an insight into the care Goldendoodle puppies require in their early days:

"The immunities puppies gain by nursing from their mother is only from the colostrum, which is what they get by nursing within the first 24-48 hours after birth. Once the colostrum is gone and mom's full milk comes in, the puppies receive no more immunity from her.

If you have to bottle feed a small puppy at birth for a few days, that puppy will not have any immunity from its mom since it missed the colostrum.

The immunity that a puppy receives from the colostrum lasts until about 6-14 weeks and is only as good as the mother's immunity, meaning if mom is not vaccinated, her puppies can't receive immunities for diseases mom hasn't been vaccinated against. Unless a titer test is done frequently on the puppy after weaning, one would not know when the puppy is losing its mom's immunity as it is different for each puppy.

A puppy doesn't need a series of vaccines, but instead, it needs a single vaccine that is given when the immunity the puppy received from mom is waning. The vaccine antibody count has to be higher than the antibody count in the puppy for the puppy's system to allow it to build its own immunity from the vaccine.

If the puppy's immunity from mom is lower than the vaccine antibody count, it will cause the puppy to build immunity from the vaccine. Vaccinating every 3-4 weeks from 8 to 16 weeks will insure a puppy builds its own immunity from one of the vaccines.

This is why a puppy should not be exposed to areas of high traffic of unknown dogs until it is 16 weeks of age as by then, at least one of the vaccines will have caused it to build its own immunity."

Photo Credit: Cherrie Mahon of River Valley Doodles

How to Pick a Puppy?

My best advice is to go with the puppy that is drawn to you. My standard strategy in selecting a pup has always been to sit a little apart from a litter and let one of the dogs come to me. My late father was, in his own way, a "dog whisperer." He taught me this trick for picking puppies, and it's never let me down.

I've had dogs in my life since childhood and enjoyed a special connection with them all. I will say that often the dog that comes to me isn't the one I might have chosen — but I still consistently rely on this method.

Having said that, Lynne Porter-Whitmire of Fountain Falls Goldendoodles adds in some words of caution: "Most puppies will be drawn to a person sitting in their play yard. The first puppy to notice will trot over. It may be the dominant puppy in the litter, one that may not be the best match for a family with young children. Possibly the most discerning puppy could be the best one for a particular couple. I like to choose puppies for families based on what they have told me. Then together we decide if a particular puppy is right for them. I have also found if there is one chocolate, or parti or white puppy in a litter, that is the one everybody wants."

You will want to choose a puppy with a friendly, easy-going temperament, and your breeder should be able to help you with your selection. Also ask the breeder about the temperament and personalities of the puppy's parents and if they have socialized the puppies.

Always be certain to ask if a Goldendoodle puppy you are interested in has displayed any signs of aggression or fear, because if this is happening at such an early age, you may experience behavioral troubles as the puppy becomes older.

Check Puppy Social Skills

When choosing a puppy out of a litter, look for one that is friendly and outgoing, rather than one who is overly aggressive or fearful. Puppies who demonstrate good social skills with their litter mates are much more likely to develop into easy-going, happy adult dogs that play well with others.

Observe all the puppies together and take notice:

Which puppies are comfortable both on top and on the bottom when play fighting and wrestling with their litter mates, and which puppies seem to only like being on top?

Which puppies try to keep the toys away from the other puppies, and which puppies share?

Which puppies seem to like the company of their litter mates, and which ones seem to be loners?

Puppies that ease up or stop rough play when another puppy yelps or cries are more likely to respond appropriately when they play too roughly as adults.

Is the puppy sociable with humans? If they will not come to you, or they display fear toward strangers, this could develop into a problem later in their life.

Is the puppy relaxed about being handled? If they are not, they may become difficult with adults and children during daily interactions, grooming or visits to the veterinarian's office.

Check Puppy's Health

Ask to see veterinarian reports to satisfy yourself that the puppy is as healthy as possible. Before making your final pick of the litter, check for general signs of good health, including the following:

1.   Breathing: will be quiet, without coughing or sneezing, and there will be no crusting or discharge around their nostrils.
2.   Body: will look round and well fed, with an obvious layer of fat over their rib cage.
3.   Coat: will be soft with no dandruff or bald spots.
4.   Energy: a well-rested puppy should be alert and energetic.
5.   Hearing: a puppy should react if you clap your hands behind their head.
6.   Genitals: no discharge visible in or around their genital or anal region.
7.   Mobility: they will walk and run normally without wobbling, limping or seeming to be stiff or sore.
8.   Vision: bright, clear eyes with no crust or discharge.

Chapter 4 – Caring for Your New Puppy

The one universal truth about any puppy is that no matter how small they are, they can find their way into big trouble.

Goldendoodle puppies are sweet, enthusiastic, happy and insatiably curious. Your first task before bringing your new pet home is to go over the house and "puppy proof" it.

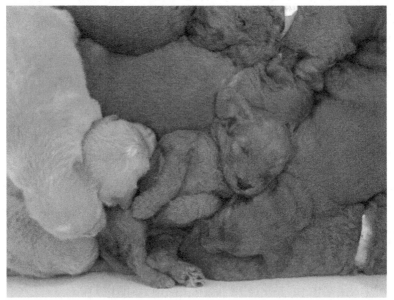

Photo Credit: Christy Stevens of Winding Creek Ranch

The Fundamentals of Puppy Proofing

If you imagine your new dog as a four-legged toddler with the inventive mind of a little genius, you will look at your home with new eyes.

Everything is a "something" to be explored and claimed, whether by sniffing, chewing, swallowing or a combination of all of the above.

Household Poisons

Dogs will eat pretty much anything. A puppy will gulp something down with no forethought, an instinct that puts them at a heightened risk for exposure to household poisons.

Go over every area to which your dog will have access, as well as the ones he can push or squeeze his way into. Remove all potential poisons from shelves and cabinets. If these are materials you need or use, get them up high out of the dog's reach or relocate them to the safety of a garage or outbuilding.

Pay particular attention to:

- cleaning products
- insecticides
- mothballs
- fertilizers
- antifreeze

Always err on the side of caution and assume that an item is poisonous. Don't leave any chemical in a place where your puppy can get into it.

Look Through Your Puppy's Eyes

A puppy will investigate anything that catches his attention, so get down on the floor at what will be his eye level. Look at things from his perspective and take the necessary precautions.

- Remove anything that dangles in an enticing way, like drapery pulls, electrical cords, frayed threads on upholstery or even bits of loose wallpaper.

- Be on the lookout for things that have fallen under your furniture or become wedged in the cushions. These "discoveries" could be potential choking hazards.

- Think about "topple" dangers. If your puppy decided to play tug of war with the coaxial cable on the back of the television, he could send the whole unit crashing down. Put the cable in a "cord minder" or otherwise secure it.

- Especially when your dog is young and in the puppy "chewing" phase, get everything stuffed out of the room that can be moved, including sofa pillows. If you have an especially prized piece of furniture, consider wrapping the legs to protect the wood.

Take every single thing out of the room that a little dog might look at as a toy. You won't believe what a determined puppy can accomplish!

Plant Dangers, Inside and Out

Everyone has some degree of understanding about indoor and outdoor plant risks, but the list is far longer than you imagine and includes numerous surprises. While you might not let your dog chew on a peach or apricot pit, do you know they can get just as sick from spinach and tomato vines?

The American Society for the Prevention of Cruelty to Animals has created a large reference list of plants for dog owners here:

http://www.aspca.org/pet-care/animal-poison-control/toxic-and-non-toxic-plants

Go through the list and get any plants out of the house that might make your dog sick. Even those that might not cause a fatal poisoning can cause severe and painful gastrointestinal upset. Don't fall into the trap of thinking a dog will leave the plants alone. The risk simply isn't worth it.

Preparing for the Homecoming

Get a travel crate in advance of your dog's arrival and a second, wire crate for use in the home. The crate is an important part of housebreaking, but it is also your best defense against separation anxiety.

In an effort to save a few dollars, new dog owners often buy a big crate, reasoning the puppy will "grow into it." Don't make this counterproductive choice! When you are teaching your dog not to "go" in the house, you will be using the crate as part of the learning process.

Animals won't soil their dens, but if you give a puppy an overly large crate, he will pick a corner to be the "bathroom." This is clearly a detriment to your housebreaking lessons. The dog will be confused about where it can and can't eliminate, increasing the number of accidents.

Crates are rated by the size of the dog in pounds / kilograms. For example, if your dog weights 40 lbs., the crate should be:

• 36" X 25" X 27" / 91.44 cm x 63.5 cm x 68.58 cm.

For a dog of 30 lbs. buy a crate that's:

• 32" X 22.5" X 24" / 81.28 cm x 57.15 cm x 60.96 cm.

It is a smart choice to buy a wire crate with adjustable

partitions, so one can have a crate that will last through adulthood.

For the ride home in the travel crate, be sure to put one or two puppy-safe chew toys inside along with a recently worn article of your clothing. The dog needs to learn your scent and associate you as the leader of his "pack." Be sure to fasten the crate securely in place with the seatbelt.

Schedule a time to pick up the puppy that is between his regular meals so he doesn't get sick in the car. Right before you put the dog in his crate, take him for a short walk so he can attend to any "business."

Photo Credit: Sharon Ruff of Ruff'n Ready Doodles

On the ride, there will be crying and whining. Don't show yourself to be a total pushover from the start. Leave the dog in the crate! For one thing, he's far safer there in the event of an accident or a sudden stop than he would be riding in someone's lap. Try taking a friend with you who can sit by the crate to be a comforting presence, but again — leave the dog in the crate! K-9 essential oils or Lavender are natural ways to calm your new puppy.

It's important not to overwhelm the puppy with too many people during this transition. If you have kids, they will naturally be excited at the prospect of having a new dog, but they shouldn't go along to bring the puppy home. The trip from the breeder needs to be calm and quiet.

Talk to your children in advance and help them to understand that the puppy is leaving his Mom and siblings. Explain that you don't want the puppy to be more frightened. Make your children see that by being quiet and letting the new dog get settled they are helping the little animal.

As soon as you get home with the puppy, take him out to relieve himself, immediately praising him for the behavior. Use a dog's "pack" instinct to your advantage. Dogs have an innate desire to please their leader, which should be you.

Take the dog to a "puppy safe" area in the house and give him a little time to explore on his own without isolating or overwhelming him. Strike a middle balance. Don't pick the puppy up every time he cries. Know in advance when his next scheduled feeding should be and put his food down on time. This immediately establishes continuity in the puppy's mind. Remember, all dogs thrive on routine.

Continue to supply the dog with worn clothing to reassure him of your role in his life. You may want to put a radio in the room playing at a low volume to keep the dog from feeling alone. At night, a warm water bottle wrapped in a soft cloth can be an enormous comfort for a puppy.

Understand that if you bring the dog to bed with you that is where he's going to want to sleep from then on. If you want a crate-trained dog, don't go down this road! Get your pet used to sleeping in his crate from the first night he is in your home. The pitiful whining may be hard to ignore, but you need to take a longer view of the situation.

The Importance of the Crate

It's almost impossible to overstate just how important the crate is in your dog's life. You are not putting your puppy in "jail" when you close the crate door. Far from it! You are giving him a secure, quiet place that is completely his! Dogs that are crate trained often go inside on their own the same way you might retreat to your room for some alone time.

Acclimating a dog to his crate circumvents separation anxiety and prepares the dog to be an excellent traveler. As you will see shortly, the crate is also crucial in the success of a quick and efficient course in housebreaking.

Don't rush the crate training or in any way create negative associations with the crate in your dog's mind. Don't get frustrated and lose your temper. At first, just leave the door open. It's actually a good idea to tie it open so it won't close by accident. Reward your puppy for going inside with treats and verbal praise.

Never use the crate as a means of punishment. When you use a crate with your dog in the correct way, it gives both you and your pet peace of mind.

Go Slow with the Children

Supervise all interactions between your children and the

puppy for everyone's safety and comfort. Make sure that your kids, especially the younger ones, know how to safely and kindly handle and carry the little dog.

The first play sessions should be limited in duration. Again, you don't want to overwhelm the puppy, especially during the first couple of days. It won't be long before your baby Goldendoodle is happily romping with the children.

What Can I Do to Make My Goldendoodle Love Me?

From the moment you bring your Goldendoodle dog home, every minute you spend with him is an opportunity to bond. The earlier you start working with your dog, the more quickly that bond will grow and the closer you and your Goldendoodle will become.

While simply spending time with your Goldendoodle will encourage the growth of that bond, there are a few things you can do to purposefully build your bond with your dog. Some of these things include:

•   Take your Goldendoodle for daily walks during which you frequently stop to pet and talk to your dog.

•   Engage your Goldendoodle in games like fetch and hide-and-seek to encourage interaction.

•   Interact with your dog through daily training sessions – teach your dog to pay attention when you say his name.

•   Be calm and consistent when training your dog – always use positive reinforcement rather than punishment.

•   Spend as much time with your Goldendoodle as possible, even if it means simply keeping the dog in the room with you while you cook dinner or pay bills.

Common Mistakes

Never pick your Goldendoodle puppy up if they are showing fear or aggression toward an object, another dog or person, because this will be rewarding them for unbalanced behavior.

If they are doing something you do not want them to continue, your puppy needs to be gently corrected by you with firm and calm energy so that they learn not to react with fear or aggression. When the mum of the litter tells her puppies off, she will use a deep noise with strong eye contact, until the puppy quickly realizes it's doing something naughty.

Don't play the "hand" game, where you slide the puppy across the floor with your hands because it's amusing for humans to see a little ball of fur scrambling to collect themselves and run back across the floor for another go.

This sort of "game" will teach your puppy to disrespect you as their leader in two different ways — first, because this "game" teaches them that humans are their play toys, and secondly, this type of "game" teaches them that humans are a source of excitement.

When your Goldendoodle puppy is teething, they will naturally want to chew on everything within reach, and this will include you. As cute as you might think it is when they are young puppies, this is not an acceptable behavior, and you need to gently, but firmly, discourage the habit, just like a mother dog does to her puppies when they need to be weaned.

Always praise your puppy when they stop inappropriate

behavior, as this is the beginning of teaching them to understand rules and boundaries. Often we humans are quick to discipline a puppy or dog for inappropriate behavior, but we forget to praise them for their good behavior.

Don't treat your Goldendoodle like a small, furry human. When people try to turn dogs into people, this can cause them much stress and confusion that could lead to behavioral problems.

A well-behaved Goldendoodle thrives on rules and boundaries, and when they understand that there is no question you are their leader and they are your follower, they will live a contented, happy and stress-free life.

Dogs are a different species with different rules; for example, they do not naturally cuddle, and they need to learn to be stroked and cuddled by humans. Therefore, be careful when approaching a dog for the first time and being overly expressive with your hands. The safest areas to touch are the back and chest — avoid patting on the head and touching the ears.

Many people will assume that a dog that is yawning is tired — this is often a misinterpretation, and instead it is signaling your dog is uncomfortable and nervous about a situation.

Be careful when staring at dogs because this is one of the ways in which they threaten each other. This body language can make them feel distinctly uneasy.

Introductions with Other Pets

As for other pets, a topic I've already touched on briefly, the whole business usually boils down to territoriality. This can depend on the temperament of both parents, as it is likely the puppies will take on not only visual but also temperament traits of one or both parents. Proper selection of breeding pairs and also the selection of puppies to retain for future breeding are critical to maintain the desired fun-loving, happy temperament typically associated with the Goldendoodle breed.

With puppies, most problems stem from the fact that "Junior" doesn't know the etiquette of interacting with older dogs or other species – in particular, cats.

Photo Credit: Bev and Arnie Eckert of Hilltop Pups

The tried and trusted bathroom "neutral zone" is the best method. The cat needs to be able to not only sniff the dog under the door, but also to just get over the affront to his dignity that you've dared bring that "creature" into his territory. Fluffy will likely put the puppy in his place when they do meet face to face.

Of course, you want to guard the little dog against any real injury, but don't overreact and start yelling. Just separate the animals. Yelling will scare the puppy and your cat will ignore you — not because he doesn't give a rip (which may indeed be the case), but because a cat's ears are attuned to softer sounds.

When you raise your voice at a cat, he no longer distinguishes your words and the message is lost. A simple, quiet, "No," or even a decided glare will go farther with Fluffy, since in the cat world, body language and eye contact are the actual basis of communication.

With other dogs in the house, take a more hands-on approach, especially if you're bringing an older Goldendoodle into the family. Two people should be present, one with each dog. It's generally best to make the first introductions in a place the older animal doesn't consider his "turf." Even for two dogs that will live in the same house, a first meeting on neutral ground is the best idea.

The dogs will pick up on your body language and tone, so just keep everything calm, friendly and happy. Let the older dog conduct the usual sniff test. If you are introducing two adult dogs, don't let this go on too long or the sniffing may be interpreted as aggression. Puppies don't understand this and often get themselves in trouble with their elders.

If this happens, the adult dog may issue a warning that comes out as a growl or snarl. This is not bad behavior on the part of the older dog. Don't punish him! He's teaching the puppy his place in the hierarchy of the home "pack."

Keeping both the new puppy and the adult dog on leashes is a good safety precaution in case puppy needs to be separated quickly from an aggressive attack.

Especially during the first weeks of this new relationship, take extra pains not to neglect the older dog. Spend time with him without the puppy present to reassure him that the bond the two of you share is still intact and strong.

Be careful at mealtimes. Always feed the dogs in separate bowls so you're not setting up a competition of the food. As for the cat's bowl, make sure it's in a private place to which the puppy has no access. If Fluffy is going to lose her temper with the dog, mealtime is certainly a hot zone for a potential alteration.

Habituation and Socialization

Habituation is when you continuously provide exposure to the same stimuli over a period of time. This will help your Goldendoodle to relax in his environment and will teach him how to behave around unfamiliar people, noises, other pets and different surroundings. Expose your Goldendoodle puppy continuously to new sounds and new environments.

When you allow for your Goldendoodle to face life's positive experiences through socialization and habituation, you're helping your Goldendoodle to build a library of valuable information that he can use when he's faced with a difficult situation. If he's had plenty of wonderful and positive early experiences, the more likely he'll be able to bounce back from any surprising or scary experiences.

When your Goldendoodle puppy arrives at his new home for the first time, he'll start bonding with his human family immediately. This will be his primary bond. His secondary bond will be with everyone outside your home. A dog should never be secluded inside his home. Be sure to find the right balance where you're not exposing your Goldendoodle puppy to too much external stimuli. If he starts becoming fearful, speak to your veterinarian.

The puppyhood journey can be tiresome yet very rewarding. Primary socialization starts between three and five weeks of age, where a pup's experiences take place within his litter. This will have a huge impact on all his future emotional behavior.

Socialization from six to twelve weeks allows for puppies to bond with other species outside of their littermates and parents. It's at this particular stage that most pet parents will bring home a puppy and where he'll soon become comfortable with humans, other pets and children.

By the time a puppy is around twelve to fourteen weeks, he becomes more difficult to introduce to new environments and new people and starts showing suspicion and distress. Nonetheless, if you've recently adopted a Goldendoodle puppy or are bringing one home and he's beyond this ideal age, don't neglect to continue the socialization process. Puppies need to be exposed to as many new situations, environments, people and other animals as possible, and it is never too late to start.

During puppyhood, you can easily teach your puppy to politely greet a new person, yet by the time a puppy has reached social maturity, the same puppy, if not properly socialized, may start lunging forward and acting aggressively, with the final outcome of lunging and nipping.

Never accidentally reward your Goldendoodle puppy for displaying fear or growling at another dog or animal by picking them up. Picking up a Goldendoodle puppy or dog at this time, when they are displaying unbalanced energy, actually turns out to be a reward for them, and you will be teaching them to continue with this type of behavior. As well, picking up a puppy literally places them in a "top dog" position where they are higher and more dominant than the dog or animal they just growled at.

The correct action to take in such a situation is to gently correct your puppy with a firm yet calm energy by distracting them with a "No," so that they learn to let you deal with the situation on their behalf.

If you allow a fearful or nervous puppy to deal with situations that unnerve them all by themselves, they may learn to react with fear or aggression, and you will have created a problem that could escalate into something quite serious as they grow older.

The same is true of situations where a young puppy may feel the need to protect themselves from a bigger or older dog that may come charging in for a sniff. It is the guardian's responsibility to protect the puppy so that they do not think they must react with fear or aggression in order to protect themselves.

Once your Goldendoodle puppy has received all their vaccinations, you can take them out to public dog parks and various locations where many dogs are found. Note that until pups have had their second shots at around 12 weeks, they are not yet fully protected with immunities.

Before allowing them to interact with other dogs or puppies, take them for a disciplined walk on leash so that they will be a little tired and less likely to immediately engage with all the other dogs.

Applying certified pure, therapeutic grade Lavender to the back paw pad before leaving the home or traveling will help calm the puppy naturally.

Keep your puppy on leash and close beside you because most puppies are usually a bundle of out-of-control energy, and you need to protect them while teaching them how far they can go before getting themselves into trouble with adult dogs who may not appreciate excited puppy playfulness.

If your puppy shows any signs of aggression or domination toward another dog, you must immediately step in and calmly discipline them.

Take your puppy everywhere with you and introduce them to many different people of all ages, sizes and ethnicities. Most people will come to you and want to interact with your puppy. If they ask if they can hold your puppy, let them, because so long as they are gentle and don't drop the puppy, this is a good way to socialize your Goldendoodle and show them that humans are friendly.

As important as socialization is, it is also important that the dog be left alone for short periods when young so that they can cope with some periods of isolation. If an owner goes out and they have never experienced this, they can destroy things or make a mess because of panic. They are thinking they are vulnerable and can be attacked by something or someone coming in to the house.

Dogs that have been socialized are able to easily diffuse a potentially troublesome situation, and hence they will rarely get into fights. Dogs that are poorly socialized often misinterpret or do not understand the subtle signals of other dogs, getting into trouble as a result.

Creating a Safe Environment

Never think for a minute that your Goldendoodle would not bolt and run away. Even well-adjusted, happy puppies and adult dogs can run away, usually in extreme conditions such as with fireworks, thunder or when scared.

Collar, tag and microchip your new Goldendoodle. Microchipping is not enough, since many pet parents tend to presume that dogs without collars are homeless or have been abandoned.

Shy and skittish Goldendoodles should have a name tag saying that they're timid so that if found, people don't presume that they've been abused or abandoned.

Photo Credit: Sharon Ruff of Ruff'n Ready Doodles

Recent photos of your Goldendoodle with the latest clip need to be placed in your wallet or purse. Goldendoodles look different as they mature and before and after a grooming or a clip. Be sure to keep an assortment of photos in a waterproof bag or safe.

Train your Goldendoodle – foster and work with a professional, positive trainer to ensure that your Goldendoodle does not run out the front door or out the backyard gate. Teach your Goldendoodle basic, simple commands such as "come" and "stay."

Create a special, fun digging area just for him, hide his bones and toys, and let your Goldendoodle know that it's okay to dig in that area. After all, dogs need to play!

Introduce your new, furry companion to all your neighbors so everyone will know that he belongs to you.

Fear Periods

Right around 10 weeks of age, puppies enter a developmental stage where they suddenly become aware that there are things out there that can cause them harm. It could be a lawn statue they've walked past every day, but suddenly they think it is going to jump out and eat them. It could be a person they have seen every day of their life while walking down the street. The possibilities are endless. You can't protect your puppy from this stage, and every dog will go through it to different degrees. This stage teaches safety, which is critical in your puppy's development. There are things you can do to help your puppy during these weeks.

The general rule of thumb during this stage is "Good experiences only." Keep things positive. Remove your puppy from any negative experience, even if this includes a person.

Do not reassure any fear. Do not talk to the dog if he is acting scared. If you do so, you think you are saying "It's okay puppy, you're okay. Nothing is going to hurt you," but puppy is hearing "Oh my gosh! That is scary! I'm worried about that too!" Puppies are pack animals. They look to a leader, and if the leader is acting composed and doesn't give any attention to the thing or person that is scaring the puppy, then you are actually telling your puppy that as leader you have assessed the situation and all is well, and silly puppy needs to get over it.

Once your puppy is composed and no longer acting scared, then you can engage in your relationship with your puppy again, but you MUST ignore them when something is causing them fear.

This stage typically lasts from 10-16 weeks, and then another similar stage is experienced again at a later age. Just remember these things during these stages, and you will greatly help your puppy. Do not reassure any fear. Remove puppy from any negative experience. Only allow positive experiences.

Puppy Nutrition

As your Goldendoodle puppy grows, manage his nutrition in graduated steps. For dogs age four months and younger, four small meals per day is appropriate. From age 4-8 months, cut this to three daily feedings. After 8 months on, two feedings, morning and evening, work best.

With puppies, the feeding times should coincide with your efforts to housebreak the dog. Do not "free feed," which is the practice of making dry food available at all times. This may be possible with an adult dog, so long as weight gain is not a problem, but puppies need regular feeding times.

Put food down for the puppy and leave it for only 10-20 minutes. Take the bowl up at the end of that time, even if some food remains. Don't give the puppy any more food until the next regularly scheduled meal.

Always use a premium, high-quality dry food. Talk to the breeder and find out what the puppy is used to eating. Replicate this food in the beginning, even if you plan to transition the dog to a different or better diet. Never make a sudden dietary switch. You will have a little dog with a majorly upset tummy. Look for puppy food labeled for the appropriate size of the puppy – small, medium or large breed.

If you want to use a new food, mix a little bit in with the existing diet, gradually increasing the amount of the new and decreasing the old over a period of about 10 days.
Never buy any kind of dog food without reading the label.

Look at the listed ingredients. You want to see meat, fishmeal and whole grains at the top. Any food that has high percentages of meat by-products and cornmeal is low in nutritional value. The food will fill the dog up, increase the amount of waste he produces, but give him few of the vitamins and minerals he needs.

Do not use wet food with a growing dog. The nutritional balance is not correct, and they are often too rich for the puppy's digestion. Also, measuring amounts is much harder with a wet food, so it's easy for your dog to be under or over fed.

Portion control is crucial. Give your dog only the amount that is listed on the package as appropriate for his weight and age. Buy stainless steel food and water bowls that are weighted to avoid the mess of tip overs. Also, the material is far superior to plastic, which retains odors and is a breeding ground for bacteria.

Placing the bowls in an elevated stand is also a good idea, and creates a better posture for the dog while he eats. If you are using an elevated surface with a puppy, make sure the little dog can easily reach the food and water.

Most stainless steel bowl sets retail for less than $25 / £14.87. Those with an included stand may be slightly higher.

Adult Nutrition

Apply the same basic guidelines to managing your adult Goldendoodle's nutritional needs. If possible, pick a product line while the dog is young and stay with the food for life. Graduated product lines make it easy to establish and maintain a nutritionally consistent feeding program that seamlessly transitions the dog first to an adult and then a senior formula.

Say No to Table Scraps!

All dogs are skilled beggars. Do not let this unhealthy habit get started! Even treats that are nutritionally formulated for your Goldendoodle should never constitute more than 5% of his daily intake of food.

On top of the potential for weight gain, many of the things we eat are toxic to dogs. Such items include, but are not limited to:

- Chocolate
- Raisins
- Alcohol
- Human vitamins (especially those with iron)
- Mushrooms
- Onions and garlic
- Walnuts
- Macadamia nuts
- Raw fish
- Raw pork
- Raw chicken
- Sugar-free gum

If you give your puppy a bone, make sure it is too large for him to swallow. Bones are both a choke and "splinter" hazard. The sharp pieces of a bone can lacerate your dog's throat and intestines. Always supervise a dog chewing on a bone, and take it away at the first sign of splintering.

I recommend against the use of animal bones, no matter how much you have been conditioned to think your dog "should" have them. Commercial chew toys rated "puppy safe" are the better option, and your dog will be just as happy.

Treats

Treats are not just for making us guilty humans feel better because we've left our dog home alone for hours, or because it makes us happy to give our pets something they really like. Today's treats are designed to improve our dog's health.

Some of us humans treat our dogs just because, others use treats for training purposes, others for health, while still others treat for a combination of reasons.

Whatever reason you choose to give treats to your Goldendoodle, keep in mind that if we treat our dogs too often throughout the day, we may create a picky eater who will no longer want to eat their regular meals.

Plus, if the treats we are giving are high calorie, we may be putting our dog's health in jeopardy by allowing them to become overweight.

Generally, the treats you feed should not make up more than approximately 10% of their daily food intake.

Photo Credit: Nathan Crockett of Best Goldendoodles

If your Goldendoodle will eat them, hard treats will help to keep their teeth cleaner.

Whatever you choose, read the labels and make sure that the ingredients are high quality and appropriately sized for your Goldendoodle.

Check any treats to see the country of origin. I would be highly suspect of anything from China, as there have been issues, including deaths from "chicken breast jerky" from China. The large pet store chains in the U.S. have decided to stop carrying many of the Chinese treats.

Soft treats are also available in a wide variety of flavors, shapes and sizes for all the different needs of our furry friends and are often used for training purposes, as they have a stronger smell.

Dental treats or chews are designed with the specific purpose of helping your Goldendoodle maintain healthy teeth and gums. They usually require intensive chewing and are often shaped with high ridges and bumps to exercise the jaw and massage gums while removing plaque build-up near the gum line.

The Canine Teeth and Jaw

Even today, too many dog food choices continue to have far more to do with being convenient for us humans to serve than they do with being a well-balanced, healthy food choice for a canine.

In order to choose the right food for your Goldendoodle, first it's important to understand a little bit about canine physiology and what Mother Nature intended when she created our furry companions.

While humans are omnivores who can derive energy from eating plants, our canine companions are carnivores, which means they derive their energy and nutrient requirements from eating a diet consisting mainly or exclusively of the flesh of animals like birds or fish.

Unlike humans, who are equipped with wide, flat molars for

grinding grains, vegetables and other plant-based materials, canine teeth are all pointed because they are designed to rip, shred and tear into meat and bone.

Another obvious consideration when choosing an appropriate food source for our furry friends is the fact that every canine is born equipped with powerful jaws and neck muscles for the specific purpose of being able to pull down and tear apart their hunted prey.

The structure of the jaw of every canine is such that it opens widely to hold large pieces of meat and bone, while the mechanics of a dog's jaw permits only vertical (up and down) movement that is designed for crushing.

The Canine Digestive Tract

A dog's digestive tract is short and simple and designed to move their natural choice of food (hide, meat and bone) quickly through their systems.

The canine digestive system is simply unable to properly break down vegetable matter, which is why whole vegetables look pretty much the same going into your dog as they do coming out the other end.

Given the choice, most dogs would never choose to eat plants and grains, or vegetables and fruits over meat, however, we humans continue to feed them a kibble-based diet that contains high amounts of vegetables, fruits and grains with low amounts of meat.

Part of this is because we've been taught that it's a healthy, balanced diet for humans, and therefore, we believe that it must be the same for our dogs, and part of this is because all the fillers that make up our dog's food are less expensive and easier to process than meat.

How much healthier and long lived might our beloved Goldendoodle be if, instead of largely ignoring nature's design for our canine companions, we chose to feed them whole, unprocessed, species-appropriate food with the main ingredient being meat?

Whatever you decide to feed your dog, keep in mind that just as too much wheat, other grains and fillers in our human diet is having a detrimental effect on our health, the same can be very true for our best fur friends.

Our dogs are also suffering from many of the same life-threatening diseases that are rampant in our human society as a direct result of consuming a diet high in genetically altered, impure, processed and packaged foods.

Photo Credit: Donna Schlosser of Suwanee Goldendoodles

The BARF Diet

Raw feeding advocates believe that the ideal diet for their dog is one that would be very similar to what a dog living in the wild would have access to, and these canine guardians are often opposed to feeding their dog any sort of commercially manufactured pet foods.

On the other hand, those opposed to feeding their dogs a raw or Biologically Appropriate Raw Food (BARF) diet believe that the risks associated with food-borne illnesses during the handling and feeding of raw meats outweigh the purported benefits.

Raw meats purchased at your local grocery store contain a much higher level of acceptable bacteria than raw food produced for dogs, because the meat purchased for human consumption is meant to be cooked, which will kill any bacteria. This means that canine guardians feeding their dogs a raw food diet can be quite certain that commercially prepared raw foods sold in pet stores will be safer than raw meats purchased in grocery stores.

Many guardians of high-energy, working breed dogs will agree that their dogs thrive on a raw or BARF diet and strongly believe that the potential benefits of feeding a dog a raw food diet are many, including:

- Healthy, shiny coats
- Decreased shedding
- Fewer allergy problems
- Healthier skin
- Cleaner teeth
- Fresher breath
- Higher energy levels
- Improved digestion
- Smaller stools

- Strengthened immune system
- Increased mobility in arthritic pets
- General increase or improvement in overall health

All dogs, whether working breed or lap dogs, are amazing athletes in their own right, therefore every dog deserves to be fed the best food available.

A raw diet is a direct evolution of what dogs ate before they became our domesticated pets and we turned toward commercially prepared, easy-to-serve dry dog food that required no special storage or preparation.

The Dehydrated Diet

Dehydrated dog food comes in both raw and cooked forms, and these foods are usually air-dried to reduce moisture to the level where bacterial growth is inhibited.

The appearance of dehydrated dog food is very similar to dry kibble, and the typical feeding methods include adding warm water before serving, which makes this type of diet both healthy for our dogs and convenient for us to serve.

Dehydrated recipes are made from minimally processed fresh whole foods to create a healthy and nutritionally balanced meal that will meet or exceed the dietary requirements for dogs.

Dehydrating removes only the moisture from the fresh ingredients, which usually means that because the food has not already been cooked at a high temperature, more of the overall nutrition is retained.

A dehydrated diet is a convenient way to feed your dog a nutritious diet, because all you have to do is add warm water and wait five minutes while the food re-hydrates so your Goldendoodle can enjoy a warm meal.

The Kibble Diet

While many canine guardians are starting to take a closer look at the food choices they are making for their furry companions, there is no mistaking that the convenience and relative economy of dry dog food kibble, which had its beginnings in the 1940s, continues to make it the most popular pet food choice for most humans.

While feeding a high-quality, bagged kibble diet that has been flavored to appeal to dogs and supplemented with vegetables and fruits to appeal to humans may keep most every Goldendoodle companion happy and healthy, you will need to decide whether this is the best diet for them.

Your Puppy's First Lessons

Dogs that are not housebroken should not have full run of the premises. Keep the puppy in a controlled area and use a baby gate to keep him there. This strategy protects your home and your pet.

Puppies face all kinds of hazards we don't even stop to consider, like staircases or drops off upper landings. Remember, little dogs have little judgment!

A baby gate does not have to be a huge investment. Depending on the size and configuration, they retail from $25-$100 / £14.87-£59.46.

If you are not home to check on your dog, put him in his crate until you return.

Housebreaking

The crate is the most essential tool at your disposal to effectively housebreak your Goldendoodle. A dog will hold his need to eliminate while he is in his "den." Crate your pet when you leave the house and take him out immediately when you return.

Set a daily routine and stick with it. All dogs respond well to such regularity, especially highly intelligent breeds like the Goldendoodle. Feed your dog at the same time and always take him out afterwards. The feeding schedule quickly comes to dictate the frequency of his need to go out. As the dog ages, the number of trips outside per day will decrease.

Be flexible about this process with a puppy. The poor little guy doesn't have full control of his bladder or bowels yet, and if he's been unusually active or over-excited, "stuff" happens.

You can expect an adult dog to need 3-4 trips out per day: waking, within an hour of eating and before bedtime. Puppies, on the other hand, go a lot! Don't ever wait more than 15 minutes to take a little dog out. You'll be sorry!

Always use encouraging phrases and positive reinforcement when a dog exhibits good elimination habits. NEVER punish a dog for having an accident. The animal is not able to associate the incident with the punishment. He will be anxious and uncomfortable because he knows he's done something to make you unhappy, but he will not understand his mistake.

If you catch the dog eliminating indoors, you can say "bad dog," but don't just go on and on about it. Keep an enzymatic cleaner on hand to eradicate both the stain and the odor.

Clean up the mess and go back to the normal routine.

I'm a big fan of Nature's Miracle Stain and Odor Removal. The product does an excellent job and is affordable at $5 / £2.97 per 32 ounce / 0.9 liter bottle.

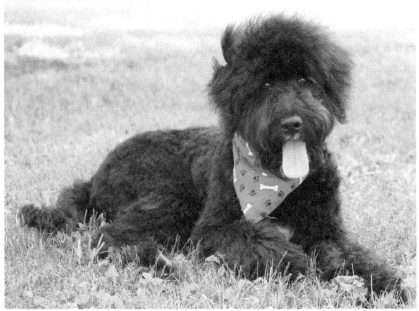

Photo Credit: Tara Mitchell of Apple Creek Doodles

The following are methods that you may or may not have considered, all of which have their own merits, including:

• Bell training
• Exercise pen training
• Crate training

All of these are effective methods, so long as you add in the one critical and often missing "wild card" ingredient, which is "human training."

When you bring home your new Goldendoodle puppy, they will be relying upon your guidance to teach them what they need to learn, and when it comes to housetraining, the first thing the human guardian needs to learn is that the puppy is not being bad when they pee or poop inside.

They are just responding to the call of Mother Nature, and you need to pay close attention right from the very beginning, because it's entirely possible to teach a puppy to go to the bathroom outside in less than a week. Therefore, if your puppy is making bathroom "mistakes," blame yourself, not your puppy.

Check in with yourself and make sure your energy remains consistently calm and patient and that you exercise plenty of compassion and understanding while you help your new puppy learn the bathroom rules. Don't clean up after your puppy with them watching, as this makes the puppy believe you are there to clean up after them, making you lower in the dog pack order.

While your puppy is still growing, on average, they can hold it approximately one hour for every month of their age. This means that if your 3-month-old puppy has been happily snoozing for two to three hours, as soon as they wake up, they will need to go outside.

Whatever methods of housebreaking you choose, ensure that the last feeding time is 4 hours or more before bedtime. Water should be picked up at least two hours before the puppy's bedtime to eliminate the chances of having accidents in the crate. Don't forget to let them out for one final potty time before placing them in the crate.

Some of the first indications or signs that your puppy needs to be taken outside to relieve themselves will be when you see them:

- sniffing around
- circling
- looking for the door
- whining, crying or barking
- acting agitated

During the early stages of potty training, adding treats as an extra incentive can be a good way to reinforce how happy you are that your puppy is learning to relieve themselves in the right place. Slowly, treats can be removed and replaced with your happy praise, or you can give your puppy a treat after they are back inside.

Next, now that you have a new puppy in your life, you will want to be flexible with respect to adapting your schedule to meet their internal clocks to quickly teach your Goldendoodle puppy their new bathroom routine.

This means not leaving your puppy alone for endless hours at a time, because firstly, they are pack animals that need companionship and your direction at all times, plus long periods alone will result in the disruption of the potty training schedule you have worked hard to establish.

If you have no choice but to leave your puppy alone for many hours, make sure that you place them in a paper-lined room or pen where they can relieve themselves without destroying your newly installed hardwood or favorite carpet. Remember, your Goldendoodle is a growing puppy with a bladder and bowels that they do not yet have complete control over.

Breeder Janet Wright of Okefeild Acres gives her advice: "We recommend using the umbilical method of training. Keeping your puppy on a leash in the house and outside of the house teaches them to stay right by you, this also helps you to keep an eye on getting them out the door for successful housebreaking. Once the puppy is obeying and coming every time you call and they are reliable to potty outside, times of freedom off of the leash can be allowed and increased over time. A short pop of the leash right when the puppy is doing wrong with an 'ah ah,' then redirection to something good is an excellent way to proactively train your puppy. This also helps to avoid your puppy becoming hand shy as you reach down to stop bad behavior."

Bell Training

A very easy way to introduce your new Goldendoodle puppy to house training is to begin by teaching them how to ring a doorbell whenever they need to go outside. A further benefit of training your puppy to ring a bell is that you will not have to listen to your puppy whining, barking or howling to be let out, and your door will not become scratched up from their nails.

Attach the bell to a piece of ribbon or string and hang it from a door handle or tape it to a doorsill near the door where you will be taking your puppy out when they need to relieve themselves. The string will need to be long enough so that your puppy can easily reach the bell with their nose or a paw.

Next, each time you take your puppy out to relieve themselves, say the word "out," and use their paw or their nose to ring the bell. Praise them for this "trick" and immediately take them outside. This type of an alert system is an easy way to eliminate accidents in the home.

Crate Training

When you train your Goldendoodle puppy to accept sleeping in their own crate at nighttime, this will also help to accelerate their potty training. Because no puppy or dog wants to relieve themselves where they sleep, they will hold their bladder and bowels as long as they possibly can.

Presenting them with familiar scents by taking them to the same spot in the yard or the same street corner will help to remind and encourage them that they are outside to relieve themselves.

Use a voice cue to remind your puppy why they are outside, such as "go pee," and always remember to praise them every time they relieve themselves in the right place, so that they quickly understand what you expect of them.

Exercise Pen Training

The exercise pen is a transition from crate-only training and will be helpful for those times when you may have to leave your Goldendoodle puppy for more hours than they can reasonably be expected to hold it.

Exercise pens are usually constructed of wire sections that you can put together in whatever shape you desire, and the pen needs to be large enough to hold your puppy's crate in one half of the pen, while the other half will be lined with newspapers or pee pads.

Place your Goldendoodle puppy's food and water dishes next to the crate and leave the crate door open (or take it off), so they can wander in and out whenever they wish to eat or drink or go to the papers or pee pads if they need to relieve themselves.

Because they are already used to sleeping inside their crate, they will not want to relieve themselves inside the area where they sleep. Therefore, your puppy will naturally go to the other half of the pen to relieve themselves on the newspapers or pee pads.

Marking Territory

Any dog, male or female, with an intact reproductive system will mark territory by urinating. This is typically an outdoor behavior, but can happen inside if the dog is upset.

Again, rely on an enzymatic cleaner to remove the odor so the dog is not attracted to the same location. This kind of territorial marking occurs most frequently with intact males. The obvious long-term solution is to have the dog neutered.

Marking territory is not the result of poor house training. The two behaviors are completely unrelated and driven by different reactions and urges.

Dealing with Separation Anxiety

Dogs express separation anxiety in a variety of ways. These include howling, barking, chewing and urinating or defecating in the house. Some behaviors, like uncontrollable jumping or nervous cowering, begin as soon as the dog recognizes you are about to leave.

The trigger may be something as simple as picking up your car keys. It's common for a dog to begin to follow you around the house trying to get your attention as his discomfort begins to grow.

You must understand before adopting a Goldendoodle that they are companion dogs who crave the companionship of their people. They rely on you as the literal center of their world and the giver of all things. When your dog exhibits separation anxiety, he isn't being "bad." He is genuinely distressed, lonely and unhappy.

Crate training is not a punishment for your dog, nor is it cruel or repressive. When you teach a dog to stay in his crate, you are giving him a "safe place." For breeds prone to separation anxiety, the crate is an essential coping mechanism. Putting your pet in his crate comforts him while you are away.

Amy Lane of Fox Creek Farm explains: "Separation anxiety isn't specific to Goldendoodles. It is something all puppies go through. Separation anxiety is more prevalent in families that are home all the time and never allow the puppy to learn to entertain him/herself. On the rare occasion the family is gone, the puppy does not know how to deal with all this alone time. New owners need to learn to balance the puppy's day with quality attention and periods of crate time to avoid creating separation anxiety issues."

Grooming

Do not allow yourself to get caught in the "my Goldendoodle doesn't like it" trap, which is an excuse many owners will use to avoid regular grooming sessions. When you allow your dog to dictate whether they will permit a grooming session, you are setting a dangerous precedent.

Once you have bonded with your dog, they love to be tickled, rubbed and scratched in certain favorite places. This is why grooming is a great source of pleasure and a way to bond with your pet.

Since there is some variation in the length and texture of the Goldendoodle coat, the type of grooming implement you will need may vary slightly. Although the breed sheds little, they still need to be fully brushed from the skin out 2-3 times a week to avoid matting and taken to the groomer 3-6 times a year (from 6 months onwards). The more wavy/curly the coat, the more brushing is needed.

- Bristle brushes are an all-purpose grooming tool suitable for short and long coats. These tools remove dirt and debris and distribute natural oils throughout the coat.

- For medium to long, curly or wooly coats, choose a wire-pin brush. They look like a series of pins stuck in a raised rubber base.

- For smoothing and detangling longer hair, a slicker brush is the best option.

(If you can find a combination, two-headed brush, you'll save a little money and be able to vary your dog's grooming sessions.)

Brushes cost less than $15 / £9 and often less than $10 / £6.

Brushing sessions have a secondary role as your chance to give your pet a quick examination for any unusual skin growths, lumps, bumps or wounds. Make sure you check around the eyes, in and behind the ears, and around the mouth.

Vigilance on your part is one of the most important aspects of your dog's long-term healthcare. Look for any signs of discharge from the eyes or nose, and check the ears for accumulated debris or a foul odor that signals the presence of parasites.

If you bathe your dog in between professional grooming sessions, take care not to get the dog's head or ears wet. Clean the head and face with a warm washcloth. Be sure to rinse all shampoo from the coat with fresh, clean water. Towel your pet dry and don't let him get cold.

I don't recommend that you try to clip your dog at home. Use a professional groomer. The risk of injuring your pet with the cutting tool is simply too great. The expense for professional grooming is approximately $25-$50 / £15-£30 per session.

How to Bathe Your Goldendoodle

The earlier you start bathing your Goldendoodle, the easier it is going to be – if your Goldendoodle gets used to it as a puppy, then he will be less difficult to handle later. Follow the tips below to bathe your Goldendoodle:

1.)   Fill a bathtub with several inches of warm water – make sure it is not too hot.
2.)   Place your Goldendoodle in the tub and wet down his coat.
3.)   Apply a dollop of tearless dog shampoo to your hands

and work it into your Goldendoodle's coat, starting at the base of his neck.

4.)   Work the shampoo into your dog's back and down his legs and tail.

5.)   Rinse your dog well, making sure to get rid of all the soap.

6.)   Towel dry your Goldendoodle to remove as much moisture as possible.

7.)   If desired, use a hair dryer on the cool setting to dry your Goldendoodle's coat the rest of the way.

Try to avoid getting water in your Goldendoodle's ears and eyes. You can follow up with putting dog ear powder in the ear to absorb any added moisture that made its way into the ear canal. Dogs with long ears trap this moisture in the ear canal, which is a great source then for bacteria to grow.

Photo Credit: Beth Engelbert of Lakeview Doodles

Nail Trimming

Even dogs that routinely walk on rough surfaces should have their nails trimmed regularly. This is a job you can do at home with an appropriate clipper. I like the kind with grips like a pair of pliers. They're easy to handle and inexpensive, selling for less than $20 / £11.88

Place the dog on an elevated surface so you can see what you're doing. Snip off the tip of each nail at a 45 degree angle, being careful not to cut into the vascular quick at the base. If you cut too far down, you'll hurt your dog and the nail will bleed heavily. If you're apprehensive about performing this chore, ask either the vet tech or the groomer to take you through the process for the first couple of times until you're confident about tackling it alone.

Anal Glands

It is quite common for a dog's anal glands to be blocked. The telltale sign is when a dog scoots or rubs its bottom on the ground or carpet. You may also notice an extremely foul odor.

To relieve the blockage, the glands must be expressed. If this is not done, an abscess may form. Since this is clearly a rather "personal" bit of maintenance, I recommend leaving this chore to your groomer or the veterinarian.

Fleas and Ticks

Fleas and ticks are generally detected while you're performing another grooming chore on your pet. Don't flip out over a few "passengers" on your dog. Neither you nor your Goldendoodle has done anything "wrong." Fleas are pretty much part of the life of having a dog. It's going to happen. When it does, you deal with it and move on.

First, do NOT put a commercial flea product on a puppy that is under 12 weeks of age. If you use such a product on an adult dog, be extremely careful. Many top selling products contain the chemical pyrethrum, which some experts claim has been linked to long-term neurological damage. I've personally not had any health-related issues but I just wanted to make you aware of this.

As an alternative to chemical products, use a standard canine shampoo and warm water to bathe your dog. Using a fine-toothed flea comb, work through the dog's coat. The tines trap any live parasites, which you will kill by submerging the comb in hot soapy water.

Wash all of the dog's bedding and any soft materials with which he has come in contact. Check all areas of the house where the dog sleeps for accumulations of "flea dirt," which is dried blood excreted by adult fleas. To make sure that there are no remaining eggs that will hatch and re-infest the dog, you need to wash these materials and surfaces daily for at least a week.

Amy Lane of Fox Creek Farm has this advice: "Dogs that get fleas will also get tapeworms as this is the life cycle of the tape worm. The flea lays eggs on the dog. The dog licks and ingests the eggs which hatch into tapeworms inside the dog. The typical monthly heartworm/deworming products do not kill tapeworms. It takes a product called Drontal to kill tapeworms."

For ticks, coat the parasite with a thick layer of petroleum jelly and wait 5 minutes. The tick will suffocate and its jaw will release, allowing you to pluck it away from the skin with a straight motion using a pair of tweezers. Don't jerk the tick off! The head will stay in place and, if the tick is still alive, continue to burrow into the skin creating a painful sore.

Collar or Harness?

Since Goldendoodles need at least 30 minutes of exercise per day, you will need the correct equipment to manage your pet on outings. This raises the question, "collar or harness?"

While the traditional collar that fits around the neck is a tried and true staple of dog ownership, I don't like to use them. I can't imagine a dog enjoys a sensation of being choked any more than I would. I prefer on-body harness restraints that look like vests.

There is a point of attachment for the lead on the back of the vest between the dog's shoulders that allows for excellent control with no pressure on the neck. I've found younger dogs to be much more accepting of this system. They strain less against the harness and behave more appropriately on walks.

I do recommend taking your dog to the store to get the right fit. These vest harnesses run large in my opinion. I've seen dogs as big as 14 lbs. / 6.35 kg take an "Extra Small" depending on their build. Regardless of size, you shouldn't have to pay more than $20 - $25 / £11.88 - £14.85.

Having said this, some breeders have a different take on it; for example, Janet Wright of Okefeild Acres says: "The careful use of a collar keeps your puppy under better control because the head is being controlled. Correction can be made immediately when they reach to do something that they shouldn't. A harness does not allow the ability to do this."

Standard Leash or Retractable?

Your choice of leash type is, for the most part, a matter of personal preference. I use both. Some grooming facilities, vet clinics and dog daycares forbid the use of retractable leads on their premises. The long lines are a trip-and-fall hazard for other human clients and an insurance nightmare.

Fixed length leashes sell for as little as $5 / £2.97, while retractable leads are less than $15 / £8.91.

Your young Goldendoodle must learn to respond to your control of the leash. Don't ever drag a dog or jerk the lead. If the dog stubbornly refuses to walk and just sits down, pick him up. It is imperative that you not allow the dog to think he is in charge of the walk.

Goldendoodles are smart and active. You want your pet to associate the sight of his lead with adventures out in the world with his human, but keep yourself in the driver's seat at all times.

Dog Walking Tips

As with all other teaching activities, reinforce good behavior from your Goldendoodle on walks by praising your pet and offering him treats when he obeys a command.

As part of the regular walking routine, teach your dog to "sit" by using the word and pointing down with your finger or the palm of your hand.

Don't attach the lead to the harness until your dog sits on command. Then wait a few seconds, keeping him in the sitting position, before saying, "Okay, let's go!"

Stop if the dog jerks or pulls on the leash. Pick him up and start the walk over with the "sit" command. Your dog will soon learn that the walk stops if he misbehaves.

Your dog's main sense is scent, which is why when you take them for a walk they spend a lot of time sniffing everything. They gather an amazing amount of information, such as being able to determine which dogs were recently in the area, their gender, their current health and age.

When two dogs meet they are likely to go up to each other and sniff near each other's jaw and then around the rear-end area.

Have you ever visited a friend and their dog has come up to you and sniffed your groin area? This may have caused some embarrassment, but this is simply a dog's way of learning about you by picking up scents.

Photo Credit: Carol McDonald of Rainbows End Puppies

The Importance of Basic Commands

A basic obedience class is a very good idea, especially for a first-time dog owner. Dogs are, by nature, eager to please. They do, however, require consistency and direction, especially in the formation of a command "language."

Dogs can learn 165-200 words, but they can't understand more than one meaning for those words. You must use the same command each time to get the desired response. If your dog barks, say "quiet." If he picks something up, use "drop it." For problem jumping, go with "down." Pick a set of words and use them over and over again. Both the word and your tone should convey your authority.

Look into enrolling your dog in an obedience class. Many big box pet stores have trainers that conduct classes in the evening. It is greatly to your advantage that Goldendoodles are highly intelligent and seem to enjoy being trained. Start the lessons early, be consistent, and you should have an extremely well-mannered companion.

Play Time and Tricks

In teaching tricks, I always suggest catering to some natural tendency the dog exhibits and then working with your pet to create extrapolations on the behavior. Goldendoodles love this kind of interaction and will add their own creative twists, turning the tables and teaching you a variation of the game.

Respond with praise and pleasure. Goldendoodles love to hear their humans laugh. The happier you seem, the faster your dog will learn. This is definitely a breed that loves toys — and destroys most of them with joyful abandon.

Don't pick soft, "shred-able" toys, including those made of rubber. The dog will swallow the pieces and a blockage can result. Avoid toys with "squeakers" for the same reason. My dogs love Nylabones, which will stand up to a lot of abuse. Most of these items cost in the $1-$5 / £0.59-£2.97 range.

Don't let your Goldendoodle have rawhide or pig's ears. Both get soft and present a choking hazard. Also avoid cow hooves. They splinter and can easily puncture the cheek or palate.

Never give puppy a rope fleece or braided fleece toy. They are very dangerous because they are easy to swallow and will not "pass." They have a high chance of requiring surgery.

Playtime is important, especially for a dog's natural desire to chase. Try channeling this instinct with toys and games. If a dog has no stimulation and has nothing to chase, they can start to chase their own tail, which can lead to problems.

Toys can be used to simulate the dog's natural desire to hunt. For example, when they catch a toy, they will often shake it and bury their teeth into it, simulating the killing of their prey.

Allow your dog to fulfill a natural desire to chew. This comes from historically catching their prey and then chewing the carcass. Providing chews or bones can prevent your dog from destroying your home.

Playing with your dog is not only a great way of getting them to use up their energy, but it is also a great way of bonding with them as they have fun. Dogs love to chase and catch balls, just make sure that the ball is too large to be swallowed.

Deer antlers are wonderful toys for Goldendoodles. Most love them. They do not smell, are all-natural and do not stain or splinter. I recommend the antlers that are not split as they last longer.

Dogs that don't get enough exercise are also more likely to develop problem behaviors like chewing, digging and barking.

Chapter 5 - Training and Problem Behaviors

Although most Goldendoodles have a reputation for being good-natured and agreeable, dogs are individuals. Any dog can develop poor behaviors. Others may be high strung or nervous, acting out in response to what they're feeling.

Behaviors that are negative in their effect are not necessarily aimed at other people. Dogs will act out aggressively at one another for some perceived breach of etiquette you may not understand at all. This can take the form of snapping, lunging, pushing, barking or baring of the teeth. All of these potential problems can be prevented with correct socialization at a young age.

Photo Credit: Donna Shaw of Donakell Goldendoodles

You not only want to enroll your pet in a training class, you also want him to be comfortable with new sights, sounds, people and places. Create opportunities in controlled environments for him to interact with other dogs. The more you work to socialize your pet, the greater your chances of having a well-mannered, flexible dog.

As a responsible dog owner, you must be attentive to the behavior of your pet as well as to what's going on in his immediate environment. You may find in a public setting that avoiding a meeting with another dog altogether is the wisest course of action. Proper leash training is crucial for taking your dog out in the world. You don't want to avoid places where you will encounter other people and dogs. The idea is to be able to take your dog to such areas without fear of incident.

Goldendoodles are happily engaged creatures. They are interested in the world around them and will thrive on seeing and doing new things. Do not shelter your pet! Help him to be a confident, self-assured dog by exposing him to well-managed outings in varied environments.

Dog Whispering

Many people can be confused when they need professional help with their dog because for many years, if you needed help with your dog, you contacted a "dog trainer" or took your dog to "puppy classes" where your dog would learn how to sit or stay.

The difference between a dog trainer and a dog whisperer would be that a "dog trainer" teaches a dog how to perform certain tasks, and a "dog whisperer" alleviates behavior problems by teaching humans what they need to do to keep their particular dog happy.

Often, depending on how soon the guardian has sought help, this can mean that the dog in question has developed some pretty serious issues, such as aggressive barking, lunging, biting or attacking other dogs, pets or people.

Dog whispering is often an emotional roller coaster ride for the humans involved that unveils many truths when they finally realize that it has been their actions (or inactions) that have likely caused the unbalanced behavior that their dog is now displaying.

Once solutions are provided, the relief for both dog and human can be quite cathartic when they realize that with the correct direction, they can indeed live a happy life with their dog.

All specific methods of training, such as "clicker training," fall outside of what every dog needs to be happy, because training your dog to respond to a clicker, which you can easily do on your own, and then letting them sleep in your bed, eat from your plate and any other multitude of things humans allow, are what makes the dog unbalanced and causes behavior problems.

I always say to people, don't wait until you have a severe problem before getting some dog whispering or professional help of some sort, because "With the proper training, Man can learn to be dog's best friend."

Rewarding Unwanted Behavior

It is very important to recognize that any attention paid to an out-of-control, adolescent puppy, even negative attention, is likely to be exciting and rewarding for your Goldendoodle puppy.

Chasing after a puppy when they have taken something they shouldn't have, picking them up when barking or showing aggression, pushing them off when they jump on other people, or yelling when they refuse to come when called are all forms of attention that can actually be rewarding for most puppies.

It will be your responsibility to provide structure for your puppy, which will include finding acceptable and safe ways to allow your puppy to vent their energy without being destructive or harmful to others.

The worst thing you can do when training your Goldendoodle is to yell at him or use punishment. Positive reinforcement training methods – that is, rewarding your dog for good behavior – are infinitely more effective than negative reinforcement – training by punishment.

It is important when training your Goldendoodle that you do not allow yourself to get frustrated. If you feel yourself starting to get angry, take a break and come back to the training session later.

Why is punishment-based training so bad? Think about it this way – your dog should listen to you because he wants to please you, right?

If you train your dog using punishment, he could become fearful of you and that could put a damper on your relationship with him. Do your dog and yourself a favor by using positive reinforcement.

Teaching Basic Commands

When it comes to training your Goldendoodle, you have to start off slowly with the basic commands. The most popular basic commands for dogs include sit, down, stay and come.

Sit

This is the most basic and one of the most important commands you can teach your Goldendoodle.

1.) Stand in front of your Goldendoodle with a few small treats in your pocket.

2.) Hold one treat in your dominant hand and wave it in front of your Goldendoodle's nose so he gets the scent.

3.) Move the treat upward and backward over your Goldendoodle's head so he is forced to raise his head to follow it.

4.) In the process, his bottom will lower to the ground. Say "Sit" only when the bottom starts to go to the ground, associating the word with the action. With any training command, say the word while the action is being done.

5.) As soon as your Goldendoodle's bottom hits the ground, praise him and give him the treat.

6.) Repeat this process several times until your dog gets the hang of it and responds consistently.

Down

After the "Sit" command, "Down" is the next logical command to teach because it is a progression from "Sit."

1.)   Kneel in front of your Goldendoodle with a few small treats in your pocket.

2.)   Hold one treat in your dominant hand and give your Goldendoodle the "Sit" command.

3.)   Reward your Goldendoodle for sitting, then give him the "Down" command.

4.)   Quickly move the treat down to the floor between your Goldendoodle's paws.

5.)   Your dog will follow the treat and should lie down to retrieve it.

6.)   Praise and reward your Goldendoodle when he lies down.

7.)   Repeat this process several times until your dog gets the hang of it and responds consistently.

Come

It is very important that your Goldendoodle responds to a "Come" command, because there may come a time when you need to get his attention and call him to your side during a dangerous situation (such as him running around too close to traffic).

1.)   Put your Goldendoodle on a short leash and stand in front of him.

2.)   Give your Goldendoodle the "Come" command, then quickly take a few steps backward away from him.

3.)   Clap your hands and act excited, but do not repeat the "Come" command.

4.)   Keep moving backwards in small steps until your Goldendoodle follows and comes to you.

5.)   Praise and reward your Goldendoodle and repeat the process.

6.)   Over time, you can use a longer leash or take your Goldendoodle off the leash entirely.

7.)   You can also start by standing further from your Goldendoodle when you give the "Come" command.

8.)   If your Goldendoodle doesn't come to you immediately, you can use the leash to pull him toward you.

Stay

This command is very important because it teaches your Goldendoodle discipline – not only does it teach him to stay, but it also forces him to listen and pay attention to you.

1.)   Find a friend to help you with this training session.

2.)   Have your friend hold your Goldendoodle on the leash while you stand in front of the dog.

3.) Give your Goldendoodle the "Sit" command and reward him for responding correctly.

4.) Give your dog the "Stay" command while holding your hand out like a "Stop" sign.

5.) Take a few steps backward away from your dog and pause for 1 to 2 seconds.

6.) Step back toward your Goldendoodle, then praise and reward your dog.

7.) Repeat the process several times, then start moving back a little further before you return to your dog.

Beyond Basic Training

Once your Goldendoodle has a firm grasp on the basics, you can move on to teaching him additional commands. You can also add distractions to the equation to reinforce your dog's mastery of the commands. The end goal is to ensure that your Goldendoodle responds to your command each and every time – regardless of distractions and anything else he might rather be doing. This is incredibly important, because there may come a time when your dog is in a dangerous situation and if he doesn't respond to your command, he could get hurt.

After your Goldendoodle has started to respond correctly to the basic commands on a regular basis, you can start to incorporate distractions.

If you previously conducted your training sessions indoors, you might consider moving them outside where your dog could be distracted by various sights, smells and sounds.

One thing you might try is to give your dog the Stay command and then toss a toy nearby that will tempt him to break his Stay. Start by tossing the toy at a good distance from him and wait a few seconds before you release him to play.

Eventually, you will be able to toss a toy right next to your dog without him breaking his Stay until you give him permission to do so.

Incorporating Hand Signals

Teaching your Goldendoodle to respond to hand signals in addition to verbal commands is very useful – you never know when you will be in a situation where your dog might not be able to hear you.

To start out, choose your dominant hand to give the hand signals, and hold a small treat in that hand while you are training your dog – this will encourage your dog to focus on your hand during training, and it will help to cement the connection between the command and the hand signal.

To begin, give your dog the Sit or Down command while holding the treat in your dominant hand and give the appropriate hand signal – for Sit you might try a closed fist, and for Down, you might place your hand flat, parallel to the ground.

When your dog responds correctly, give him the treat. You will need to repeat this process many times in order for your dog to form a connection between both the verbal command and the hand signal with the desired behavior.

Eventually, you can start to remove the verbal command from the equation – use the hand gesture every time, but start to use the verbal command only half the time.

Once your dog gets the hang of this, you should start to remove the food reward from the equation. Continue to give your dog the hand signal for each command, and occasionally use the verbal command just to remind him.

You should start to phase out the food rewards, however, by offering them only half the time. Progressively lessen the use of the food reward, but continue to praise your dog for performing the behavior correctly so he learns to repeat it.

Photo Credit: Bart Hainz of Heartland Goldens and Mini Goldendoodles

Teaching Distance Commands

In addition to getting your dog to respond to hand signals, it is also useful to teach him to respond to your commands even when you are not directly next to him. This may come in handy if your dog is running around outside and gets too close to the street – you should be able to give him a Sit or Down command so he stops before he gets into a dangerous situation.

Teaching your dog distance commands is not difficult, but it does require some time and patience.

To start, give your Goldendoodle a brief refresher course of the basic commands while you are standing or kneeling right next to him.

Next, give your dog the Sit and Stay commands, then move a few feet away before you give the Come command.

Repeat this process, increasing the distance between you and your dog before giving him the Come command. Be sure to praise and reward your dog for responding appropriately when he does so.

Once your dog gets the hang of coming on command from a distance, you can start to incorporate other commands.

One method of doing so is to teach your dog to sit when you grab his collar. To do so, let your dog wander freely and every once in a while walk up and grab his collar while giving the Sit command.

After a few repetitions, your dog should begin to respond with a Sit when you grab his collar, even if you do not give the command.

Gradually, you can increase the distance from which you come to grab his collar and give him the command.

After your dog starts to respond consistently when you come from a distance to grab his collar, you can start giving the Sit command without moving toward him.

It may take your dog a few times to get the hang of it, so be patient. If your dog doesn't sit right away, calmly walk up to him and repeat the Sit command, but do not grab his collar this time.

Eventually, your dog will get the hang of it, and you can start to practice using other commands like Down and Stay from a distance.

Clicker Training

When it comes to training your Goldendoodle, you are going to be most successful if you maintain consistency. Goldendoodles usually are cooperative and easy to train, although some can be stubborn, so unless you are very clear with your dog about what your expectations are, he may simply decide not to follow your commands.

A simple way to achieve consistency in training your Goldendoodle is to use the principles of clicker training. Clicker training involves using a small handheld device that makes a clicking noise when you press it between your fingers.

Clicker training is based on the theory of operant conditioning, which helps your dog to make the connection between the desired behavior and the offering of a reward.

Goldendoodles have a natural desire to please, so if they learn that a certain behavior earns your approval, they will be eager to repeat it – clicker training is a great way to help your dog quickly identify the particular behavior you want him to repeat.

All you have to do is give your Goldendoodle a command and, as soon as he performs the behavior, you use the clicker. After you use the clicker, give your dog the reward as you would with any form of positive reinforcement training.

Some of the benefits of clicker training include:

•   Very easy to implement – all you need is the clicker.

•   Helps your dog form a connection between the command and the desired behavior more quickly.

•   You only need to use the clicker until your dog makes the connection, then you can stop.

•   May help to keep your dog's attention more effectively if he hears the noise.

Clicker training is just one method of positive reinforcement that you can consider for training your Goldendoodle.

No matter what method you choose, it is important that you maintain consistency and always praise and reward your dog for responding to your commands correctly, so he learns to repeat the behavior.

First Tricks

When teaching your Goldendoodle their first tricks, in order to give them extra incentive, find a small treat that they would do anything to get, and give the treat as a reward to help solidify a good performance.

Most dogs will be extra attentive during training sessions when they know that they will be rewarded with their favorite treats.

If your Goldendoodle is less than six months old when you begin teaching them tricks, keep your training sessions short (no more than 5 or 10 minutes) and make the sessions lots of fun.

As your Goldendoodle becomes an adult, you can extend your sessions, because they will be able to maintain their focus for longer periods of time.

Photo Credit: Janet Wright of Okefeild Acres

Shake a Paw

Who doesn't love a dog who knows how to shake a paw? This is one of the easiest tricks to teach your Goldendoodle.

Practice every day until they are 100% reliable with this trick, and then it will be time to add another trick to their repertoire.

Most dogs are naturally either right or left pawed. If you know which paw your dog favors, ask them to shake this paw. Find a quiet place to practice, without noisy distractions or other pets, and stand or sit in front of your dog. Place them in the sitting position and hold a treat in your left hand.

Say the command "Shake" while putting your right hand behind their left or right paw and pulling the paw gently toward yourself until you are holding their paw in your hand. Immediately praise them and give them the treat.

Most dogs will learn the "Shake" trick very quickly, and in no time at all, once you put out your hand, your Goldendoodle will immediately lift their paw and put it into your hand, without your assistance or any verbal cue.

Roll Over

You will find that just like your Goldendoodle is naturally either right or left pawed, that they will also naturally want to roll either to the right or the left side.

Take advantage of this by asking your dog to roll to the side they naturally prefer. Sit with your dog on the floor and put them in a lie down position.

Hold a treat in your hand and place it close to their nose without allowing them to grab it, and while they are in the lying position, move the treat to the right or left side of their head so that they have to roll over to get to it.

You will quickly see which side they want to naturally roll to; once you see this, move the treat to that side. Once they roll over to that side, immediately give them the treat and praise them. You can say the verbal cue "Over" while you demonstrate the hand signal motion (moving your right hand in a half circular motion) from one side of their head to the other.

Sit Pretty

While this trick is a little more complicated, and most dogs pick up on it very quickly, remember that this trick requires balance, and every dog is different, so always exercise patience.

Find a quiet space with few distractions and sit or stand in front of your dog and ask them to "Sit."

Have a treat nearby (on a countertop or table) and when they sit, use both of your hands to lift up their front paws into the sitting pretty position, while saying the command "Sit Pretty." Help them balance in this position while you praise them and give them the treat.

Once your Goldendoodle can do the balancing part of the trick quite easily without your help, sit or stand in front of your dog while asking them to "Sit Pretty" and hold the treat above their head, at the level their nose would be when they sit pretty.

If they attempt to stand on their back legs to get the treat, you may be holding the treat too high, which will encourage them to stand up on their back legs to reach it. Go back to the first step and put them back into the "Sit" position and again lift their paws while their backside remains on the floor.

The hand signal for "Sit Pretty" is a straight arm held over your dog's head with a closed fist. Place your Goldendoodle beside a wall when first teaching this trick so that they can use the wall to help their balance.

A young Goldendoodle puppy should be able to easily learn these basic tricks before they are six months old, and when you are patient and make your training sessions short and fun for your dog, they will be eager to learn more.

Excessive Jumping

Don't let excessive jumping get started. This is an out-of-control behavior that will earn your dog a bad reputation very quickly. A dog that knocks people or things over isn't going to be welcome, even if the animal is just expressing enthusiasm. Larger Goldendoodles could easily injure a small child or a frail person, and jumping is the number one behavior that people who are afraid of dogs say they find to be threatening.

It's also a mistake to think that all excessive jumping is enthusiastic happiness. You may have a really dominant dog on your hands who is telling you clearly, "I'm in charge." A dog who knows where he stands in the hierarchy of the pack is not going to jump on someone more dominant than himself — which should be all humans. Many "jumpers" see themselves as the "top dog" in all situations.

Photo Credit: Renee Sigman of Yesteryear Acres

You are your dog's master. Sternly enforce the "no jumping" rule. Anything else will confuse your pet. Dogs understand the concept of space. Don't retreat from a jumping dog. Step sideways and forward. Take back the space your pet is trying to claim.

Don't try to knock the dog down, but don't be surprised if he careens into you and stumbles. Stay casual, calm and confident. Move slowly and deliberately. Take complete charge of the "bubble" around your body and don't let the dog invade your territory.

Your jumper won't be expecting this response from you, and he won't like it. After pushing the point through several failed attempts, he will ultimately lose interest and give up when his dominant message is not being accepted.

Barking Behavior

Barking is such a serious problem it can be responsible for outright wars with the neighbors or an eviction notice from your landlord. In order to stop problem barking, you have to figure out why the dog is raising the roof.

Is he lonely? bored? excited? anxious? Is the barking a response to something he's seeing? hearing? smelling?

First, approach the excessive barking with patience and consistency. If a firm "No" or "Quiet" doesn't work, some owners use a plant mister or squirt gun as negative reinforcement. Aim for the face, but be careful not to let the stream hit the eyes. Your goal is only to startle your pet, get his attention and associate a negative with the problem behavior. In addition, using "Bitter Apple" brand spray directly into the mouth will teach the puppy not to bark.

If none of these methods work, consider a humane bark collar that releases a harmless spray of citronella into the dog's nose. The unit fires in response to vibrations in the animal's throat. Although somewhat expensive at $100/£60, the system works in almost all cases.

Chewing

Chewing is a natural behavior. Done to excess, it indicates boredom and anxiety. Address the likely cause by spending more time with your pet and getting him out of the house daily, but also redirect his chewing behavior toward proper toys like Nylabones. If you do find your dog gnawing on an inappropriate item, reprimand him, confiscate the object and give him an acceptable chew toy.

Digging

Digging, like the other problem behaviors I've been discussing, is an expression of fear, anxiety and/or boredom. Your dog is literally trying to dig his way out to go find you! An out-of-control digger can destroy your furniture and even claw right through a door.

If increasing the dog's exercise time and giving him more attention doesn't help, consider taking your Goldendoodle to a dog daycare facility so he won't be alone during the day while you're at work.

Begging

The trick to stopping a dog from begging at the table is to never let him get started in the first place! Make "people" food off limits from day one and don't cheat!

If necessary, put your dog in another part of the house during meal times. As a control measure, this one applies to you almost more than to the dog. If you can't ignore a plaintive, begging set of Goldendoodle eyes, then the dog isn't the only one in need of discipline!

Chasing

Goldendoodles are excellent runners. If you're not careful, your dog will answer his instinctual urge to chase things and put himself in great danger, especially in busy urban areas.

Keep your pet leashed at all times. Never allow your Goldendoodle off the lead unless you are securely inside a fenced area. A dog may become so concentrated on the chase, he won't come when he's called.

Biting

April Cliber of Cliberdoodle advises on dealing with nipping behavior: "All puppies go through a nipping phase. It can be painful and frustrating! The good news is that is DOES pass. Ignoring and redirecting is the best way to get through it. If puppy is being nippy while you are petting, try giving him a chew toy to put in his mouth and see if he will 'hold' it. When young kids get frustrated tell them to walk away. If (when) puppy follows, instruct them to get on the couch where they can't be reached.

Puppies tend to nip more when they are overtired. Sometimes a nap in the crate is best. With no fuss, just place him in the crate and walk away. Yelling or scolding won't be helpful. Redirection is the key. They really don't understand why you are mad. Withholding attention is the best way for puppy to understand a behavior is unwanted. Good behavior should always be met with affection and a happy voice."

Chapter 6 – Goldendoodle Health

Although your veterinarian is your dog's primary physician, you are your pet's real healthcare provider on a daily basis. No one will ever know your dog better than you do, or have your ability to judge what is "normal." Even if there is no obvious injury or illness, if you have the sense that something is wrong, get your dog checked out. The more that you understand preventive healthcare, the more finely tuned your senses will be in this matter.

Photo Credit: Cherrie Mahon of River Valley Doodles

Your Veterinarian Is Your Partner

Finding a qualified veterinarian is a crucial first step in dog ownership. If you do not already have a vet, ask your breeder, friends, or family for recommendations or contact your local dog club for referrals.

Your first trip to the vet should be solo. Your purpose is to meet the doctor and evaluate the facility. Be clear about this when you call and make the appointment, and express your desire to pay for a regular office visit. Do not waste anyone's time when you get there. Have your questions ready, and make sure the following points are covered:

- How long has this practice been open?
- How many vets work here?
- Are any of those doctors specialists?
- If so, in what area?
- If not, to whom do you refer patients?
- What are your regular business hours?
- Are you affiliated with an emergency clinic?
- Do you have emergency hours?
- What specific services do you offer?
- Do you have or can you recommend a groomer?
- May I have an estimated schedule of fees?
- Do you currently treat any Goldendoodles?

Pay attention to everything you see and hear. Develop an impression of the doctor, the facility and the staff. Look for:

- the manner of the staff with other clients
- how organized the office seems to be
- evidence of engagement with the clientele (office bulletin board, cards and photos displayed, etc.)
- the quality of all visible equipment
- the state of the waiting area and back rooms
- prominent display of doctors' credentials

Above all, go with your own "gut." You will know almost immediately if the place "feels" right. Trust that intuition. If you get a bad feeling, even in a modern and well-appointed clinic, check out other practices before settling on a vet.

Your Dog's First Visit to the Vet

When you pick a vet, make a second appointment to go in with your Goldendoodle. At that time, take in the puppy's medical records. Be prepared to talk about finishing the recommended vaccinations and scheduling a time to have your dog spayed or neutered. Expect the usual routine procedures:

- temperature
- a check of the heart and lungs (using a stethoscope)
- taking the dog's weight
- measuring the puppy

Vets take these baseline numbers to chart a dog's growth and physical progress. If you have specific questions or concerns, prepare them in advance. Write these things down so you don't forget. You may be more nervous than your puppy!

Vaccinations

Recommended vaccinations begin at 6-7 weeks and include distemper, hepatitis, parvovirus, parainfluenza and adenovirus 2. Boosters will be set at 9, 12 and 16 weeks. In some areas, a vaccine for Lyme disease starts at 16 weeks with a booster at 18 weeks. The rabies vaccination is administered at 12-16 weeks and then yearly for life.

Evaluating for Worms

When you acquire a puppy from a breeder, it's rare for the dog to have parasites, but worms are more common in rescue dogs and strays. Roundworms look like small white granules around the anus. Other types of worms can only be seen through a microscope.

Since some parasites, like tapeworms, may be life threatening, these tests are important and do not reflect on your perceived care of the dog. If the puppy tests positive, the standard treatment is a deworming agent with a follow-up dose in 10 days.

Spaying and Neutering

Unlike purebred adoption, the owners of crossbreeds like the Goldendoodle can choose whether or not to have their pet spayed or neutered. I recommend you decide in favor of the procedure. Altering a companion animal not only eliminates unwanted pregnancies, the surgeries also offer significant associated health benefits.

In male dogs, neutering reduces the risk of prostatic disease and perianal tumors while lessening aggressive behaviors, territorial instincts, urine marking and inappropriate mounting.

In spayed females there is less risk for breast cancer and no prospect of uterine or ovarian cancer. Also, alleviating hormonal surges takes care of the mood swings typical of a female dog in heat.

"Normal" Health Issues

Goldendoodles are vigorous, healthy dogs, but like all canines, they can face medical issues. The following are "normal" health-related matters that may need veterinary evaluation.

Pets that are inattentive or lethargic and that are not eating or drinking should always be examined by a veterinarian. None of these behaviors are normal for a healthy Goldendoodle.

Diarrhea

Goldendoodle puppies are subject to digestive upsets. Puppies will just get into things they shouldn't, like human food or even the kitchen garbage. Diarrhea from these causes resolves within 24 hours.

During that time, the puppy should have only small portions of dry food and no treats. Give the dog lots of fresh, clean water to guard against dehydration. If the loose, watery stools are still present after 24 hours, take your Goldendoodle to the vet.

Photo Credit: Melissa Farmer of Farmer Doodles

The same period of watchful waiting applies for adult dogs. If episodic diarrhea becomes chronic, take a good look at your pet's diet.

Chances are good the dog is getting too much rich, fatty food and needs less fat and protein. Some dogs also do better eating small amounts of food several times a day rather than having 2-3 larger meals.

Allergy testing can identify the causes of some cases of diarrhea. Many small dogs are allergic to chicken and turkey. A change in diet resolves their gastrointestinal upset immediately. Diets based on rabbit or duck are often used for dogs with such intolerances. Either a bacteria or a virus can cause diarrhea, which accompanies fever and vomiting. Parasites, in particular tapeworms and roundworms, may also be to blame.

Janet Wright of Okefeild Acres observes: "Diarrhea can be caused by puppies being under stress when going to their new home. In addition to a lower protein diet, the addition of plain Greek yoghurt or pure canned pumpkin can help firm the stools. Stress can make bacteria multiply in the intestines. The use of essential oils has been a big help in our kennel; we give samples of those to administer to pups as they adjust to their new home environment."

Vomiting

Dietary changes or the puppy "getting into something" can also cause vomiting. Again, this should resolve within 24 hours. If the dog tries to vomit but can't bring anything up, vomits blood or can't keep water down, take your pet to the vet immediately.

Dehydration from vomiting occurs faster than in a case of diarrhea and can be fatal. It is possible that your dog may need intravenous fluids.

When your dog is vomiting, always have a good look around to identify what, if anything, the dog may have chewed and swallowed. This can be a huge benefit in targeting appropriate treatment. Other potential culprits include: hookworm, roundworm, pancreatitis, diabetes, thyroid disease, kidney disease, liver disease or a physical blockage.

Bloat

Any dog can suffer from bloat, but some are at higher risk than others. Also known as gastric dilation/volvulus or GDV, bloat cannot be treated with an antibiotic or prevented with a vaccine. If left untreated, the condition can be fatal.

In severe cases, the stomach twists partially or completely. This causes circulation problems throughout the digestive system. Dogs that do not receive treatment go into cardiac arrest. Even if surgical intervention is attempted, there is no guarantee of success.

Signs of bloat are often mistaken for indications of excess gas. The dog may salivate and attempt to vomit, pace and whine. Gas reduction products at this stage can be helpful. As the stomach swells, it places pressure on surrounding vital organs, and may burst. All cases of bloat are a *serious* medical emergency.

Risk Factors

Larger dogs with deep chests and small waists face a greater risk of developing bloat. These include the Great Dane, Weimaraner, Saint Bernard, Irish Setter and the Standard Poodle.

Eating habits also factor into the equation. Dogs that eat one large meal per day consisting of dry food are in a high-risk category. Feed three small meals throughout the day. This helps to prevent gulping, which leads to ingesting large amounts of air.

Experts recommend dry food for dogs, but don't let your pet drink lots of water after eating. Doing so causes the dry food in the stomach to expand, leading to discomfort, and a dilution of the digestive juices.

Limit the amount of play and exercise after meals. A slow walk promotes digestion, but a vigorous romp can be dangerous.

Stress also contributes to bloat, especially in anxious or nervous dogs. Changes in routine, confrontations with other dogs and moving to a new home can all trigger an attack.

Dogs between the ages of 4 and 7 are at an increased risk. Bloat occurs most often between 2 a.m. and 6 a.m., roughly 10 hours after the animal has had his dinner.

Prevention

Feed your pet small meals 2-3 times a day, limiting both water intake and exercise after eating. Take up your pet's water at mealtime and do not offer it to the dog for at least 30 minutes after your pet finishes his meal. Do not allow strenuous activity for at least an hour.

Test your dog's dry food by putting a serving in a bowl with water. Leave the material to expand overnight. If the degree of added bulk seems excessive, consider switching to a premium or organic food.

Keep an anti-gas medicine with simethicone on hand. (Consult with your veterinarian on correct dosage.) Consider adding a probiotic to your dog's food to reduce gas in the stomach and to improve digestive health. If a dog experiences bloat once, his risk of a future episode is greater. Keep copies of his medical records at home and know the location of the nearest emergency vet clinic.

Allergies

Like humans, dogs suffer from allergies. Food, airborne particles and materials that touch the skin can all cause reactions. Owners tend to notice changes in behavior that suggest discomfort, like itching. Common symptoms include chewing or biting of the tail, stomach or hind legs, or licking of the paws.

In reaction to inhaled substances, the dog will sneeze, cough or experience watering eyes. Ingested substances may lead to vomiting or diarrhea. Dogs can also suffer from rashes or a case of hives. Your poor Goldendoodle can be just as miserable as you are during an allergy attack.

If the reaction occurs in the spring or fall, the likely culprit is seasonal pollen or, in the case of hot weather, fleas. Food additives like beef, corn, wheat, soybeans and dairy products can all cause gastrointestinal upset.

As with any allergy, take away suspect items or try a special diet. Allergy testing offers a definitive diagnosis and pinpoints necessary environmental and dietary changes. The tests are expensive, costing $200+ / £120+. The vet may recommend medication or bathing the dog in cool, soothing water. Special diets are also extremely helpful. Be aware that allergies can often be diagnosed when the problem is really a yeast issue.

For acne-like chin rashes, switch to stainless steel, glass or ceramic food dishes. Plastic feeding dishes cause this rash, which looks like blackheads surrounded by inflamed skin.

Wash the dog's face in clear, cool water and ask the vet for an antibiotic cream to speed the healing process.

Photo Credit: Candice Farrell of Ooodles of Doodles

General Signs of Illness

Any of the following symptoms can point to a serious medical problem. Have your pet evaluated for any of these behaviors. Don't wait out of fear that you are just being an alarmist. Vets can resolve most medical problems in dogs if treatment starts at the first sign of illness.

Coughing and/or Wheezing

Occasional coughing is not a cause for concern, but if it goes on for more than a week, a vet visit is in order. A cough may indicate:

- kennel cough
- heartworm
- cardiac disease

- bacterial infections
- parasites
- tumors
- allergies

The upper respiratory condition called "kennel cough" presents with a dry, hacking cough. It is a form of canine bronchitis caused by warm, overcrowded conditions with poor ventilation. In most cases, kennel cough resolves on its own.

Consult with your veterinarian. The doctor may prescribe a cough suppressant or suggest the use of a humidifier to soothe your pet's irritated airways. When the cause of a cough is unclear, the vet will take a full medical history and order tests, including blood work and X-rays. Fluid may also be drawn from the lungs for analysis. Among other conditions, the doctor will be attempting to rule out heartworms.

A Note on Heartworms

Mosquitoes spread heartworms (*Dirofilaria Immitis*) through their bites. They are thin, long parasites that infest the muscles of the heart, where they block blood vessels and cause bleeding. Their presence can lead to heart failure and death.

Coughing and fainting, as well as an intolerance to exercise are all symptoms of heartworm. Discuss heartworm prevention with your vet and decide on the best course of action to keep your pet safe.

Other Warning Signs

Additional warning signs include:

- excessive and unexplained drooling
- excessive consumption of water and increased urination
- changes in appetite leading to weight gain or loss
- marked change in levels of activity
- disinterest in favorite activities
- stiffness and difficulty standing or climbing stairs
- sleeping more than normal
- shaking of the head
- any sores, lumps or growths
- dry, red or cloudy eyes

Often the signs of serious illness are subtle. Trust your instincts. If you think something is wrong, do not hesitate to consult with your vet.

Diabetes

Canines can suffer from three types of diabetes: insipidus, diabetes mellitus and gestational diabetes. All point to malfunctioning endocrine glands and are often linked to poor diet. Larger dogs are in a higher risk category.

- In cases of diabetes insipidus, low levels of the hormone vasopressin create problems with the regulation of blood glucose, salt and water.

- Diabetes mellitus is more common and dangerous. It is divided into Types I and II. Type I first develops in young dogs and may be referred to as "juvenile." Type II is more prevalent in adult and older dogs.

- Gestational diabetes occurs in pregnant female dogs and requires the same treatment as diabetes mellitus. Obese dogs are at greater risk.

Abnormal insulin levels interfere with blood sugar levels. Poodles face a high risk for diabetes, a predisposition that can be passed into Goldendoodles. In general, though, crossbred dogs have shown more resistance to the condition.

Symptoms of Canine Diabetes

All of the following behaviors are signs that a dog is suffering from canine diabetes:

- excessive water consumption
- excessive and frequent urination
- lethargy / uncharacteristic laziness
- weight gain or loss for no reason

It is possible your pet may display no symptoms whatsoever. Diabetes can be slow to develop, so the effects may not be immediately noticeable. Regular check-ups help to catch this disease, which can be fatal even when you do not realize that anything is wrong.

Managing Diabetes

As part of a diabetes management program, the vet will recommend diet changes, including special food. Your dog may need insulin injections. Although this may sound daunting, your vet will train you to administer the shots. A dog with diabetes can live a full and normal life. Expect regular visits to the vet to check for heart and circulatory problems.

Dental Care

Chewing is a dog's only means of maintaining his teeth. Many of our canine friends develop dental problems early in life because they don't get enough of this activity. Not all dogs are prone to cavities. Most do suffer from accumulations of plaque and associated gum diseases. Often, severe halitosis (bad breath) is the first sign that something is wrong.

With dental problems, gingivitis develops first and, if unaddressed, progresses to periodontitis. Warning signs of gum disease include:

- a reluctance to finish meals
- extreme bad breath
- swollen and bleeding gums
- irregular gum line
- plaque build-up
- drooling, and/or loose teeth

The smaller Poodle varieties are prone to gingivitis, which places some Goldendoodles at a higher risk as well.

The bacterial gum infection periodontitis causes inflammation, gum recession and possible tooth loss. It requires treatment with antibiotics to prevent a spread of the infection to other parts of the body. Symptoms include:

- pus at the gum line
- loss of appetite
- depression
- irritability
- pawing at the mouth
- trouble chewing
- loose or missing teeth
- gastrointestinal upset

Treatment begins with a professional cleaning. This procedure may also involve root work, descaling and even extractions.

With Proliferating Gum Disease, the gums overgrow the teeth causing inflammation and infection. Other symptoms include:

- thickening and lengthening of the gums
- bleeding
- bad breath
- drooling
- loss of appetite

The vet will prescribe antibiotics, and surgery is usually required.

Photo Credit: Janece Schommer of Goldendoodle Acres

Home Dental Care

There are many products available to help with home dental care for your Goldendoodle. Some owners opt for water additives that break up tartar and plaque, but in some cases dogs experience stomach upset. Dental sprays and wipes are also an option, but so is a gentle gum massage to help break up plaque and tartar.

Most owners incorporate some type of dental chew in their standard care practices. Greenies Dental Chews for Dogs are popular and well tolerated in a digestive sense. An added plus is that dogs usually love them. The treats come in different sizes and are priced in a range of $7 / £4.21 for 22 "Teeny Greenies" and $25 / £15 for 17 Large Greenies.

Brushing your pet's teeth is the ultimate defense for oral health. This involves the use of both a canine-specific toothbrush and toothpaste. Never use human toothpaste, which contains fluoride toxic to your dog. Some dog toothbrushes resemble smaller versions of our own, but I like the models that just fit over your fingertip. I think they offer greater control and stability.

The real trick to brushing your pet's teeth is getting the dog comfortable with having your hands in his mouth. Start by just massaging the dog's face, and then progressing to the gums before using the toothbrush. In the beginning, you can even just smear the toothpaste on the teeth with your fingertip.

Try to schedule these brushing sessions for when the dog is a little tired, perhaps after a long walk. Don't apply pressure, which can stress the dog. Just move in small circular motions and stop when the Goldendoodle has had enough of the whole business. If you don't feel you've done enough, stop. A second session is better than forcing your dog to do something he doesn't like and creating a negative association in his mind.

Even if you do practice a full home dental care routine, don't scrimp on annual oral exams in the vet's office. Exams not only help to keep the teeth and gums healthy, but also to check for the presence of possible cancerous growths.

The Matter of Genetic Abnormalities

The Goldendoodle gene pool does contain known genetic diseases. Golden Retrievers develop hip and elbow dysplasia. They can suffer from eye problems, including progressive retinal atrophy, cataracts and retinal dysplasia.

Poodles are susceptible to hip dysplasia, progressive renal atrophy and Von Willebrand's disease. The bleeding disorder Von Willebrand's is comparable to hemophilia in humans. It is an incurable condition that prevents proper blood clotting.

Any of these conditions can affect Goldendoodles, and not all are identifiable in puppies. For this reason, you are well advised to ask about health testing of the parents and the puppies used to create the cross.

Rare conditions in Goldendoodles include the endocrine disorder Addison's Disease and Sebaceous Adenitis, a malfunction of the skin's oil-producing glands.

If you are dealing with a casual breeder, advanced health screenings are rare. A kennel owner with an organized breeding program should be able to discuss the topic with you at length. Beware of breeders claiming such tests are unnecessary or who say none of their dogs have ever had a genetic condition.

In addition to health testing, ask how long the breeder has had the dog(s) and what they have produced. A good breeder will keep back their own puppies to use for breeding when they know that they are producing puppies that have been proven to be healthy over a period of years. Hip dysplasia can be brought on by different environmental circumstances, overfeeding, growing too fast by a high protein diet and running on hard surfaces (especially before growth plates are closed.)

Luxating Patella

A dog with a luxating patella experiences frequent dislocations of the kneecap. The condition is common in small and miniature breeds, and can affect one or both kneecaps. Surgery may be required to rectify the problem. Often owners have no idea anything is wrong with their dog's knee joint. Then the pet jumps off a bed or leaps to catch a toy, lands badly and begins to limp and favor the leg.

The condition may be genetic in origin, so it is important to ask a breeder if the problem has surfaced in the line of dogs he cultivates. A luxating patella can also be the consequence of a physical injury, especially as a dog ages. For this reason, you may want to discourage jumping in older dogs. Offer steps in key locations around the home to help your senior Goldendoodle navigate in safety.

Any time you see your dog limping or seeming more fatigued than usual after vigorous play, have the dog checked out. Conditions like a luxating patella only get worse with time and wear, and need immediate treatment.

Hip Dysplasia

Goldendoodles may also be susceptible to hip dysplasia. This defect prevents the thighbone from fitting into the hip joint. It is a painful condition that causes limping in the hindquarters. Again, this may be inherited, or the consequence of injury and aging.

When hip dysplasia presents, the standard treatment is anti-inflammatory medication. Some cases need surgery and even a full hip replacement. Surgical intervention for this defect carries a high success rate, allowing your dog to live a full and happy life.

Canine Arthritis

Dogs, like humans, can suffer from arthritis. This debilitating degeneration of the joints often affects larger breeds. As the cartilage in the joints breaks down, the action of bone rubbing on bone creates considerable pain. In turn, the animal's range of motion becomes restricted.

Standard treatments do not differ from those used for humans. Aspirin addresses pain and inflammation, while supplements like glucosamine work on improving joint health. Environmental aids, like steps and ramps, ease the strain on the affected joints and help pets stay active.

Arthritis is a natural consequence of aging. Management focuses on making your pet comfortable and facilitating ease of motion. Some dogs become so crippled that their humans buy mobility carts for them. These devices, which attach to the hips, put your pooch on wheels. Goldendoodles adapt well under such circumstances. So long as your pet is otherwise healthy, this is a reasonable approach to a debilitating, but not fatal ailment.

Often called "dog wheelchairs," you can buy these units online from sites like:

- www.handicappedpets.com
- www.k9carts.com
- www.eddieswheels.com

Although the carts are adjustable, having your dog custom fitted for the appliance may provide more mobility.

Photo Credit: Bobbie Yoder of Little Mountain Doodles

Canine Eye Care

Check your dog's eyes on a regular schedule to avoid problems like clogged tear ducts. Also, many dogs suffer from excessive tearing, which can stain the fur around the eyes and down the muzzle. This is a problem with Poodles and can occur in Goldendoodles with lighter coats.

As a part of good grooming, keep the corners of your pet's eyes and the muzzle free of mucus to prevent bacterial growth.

If your dog is prone to mucus accumulation, ask your vet for a sterile eyewash or gauze pads. Also consider having the dog tested for environmental allergies.

Take the precaution of keeping the hair well-trimmed around

your pet's eyes. If you do not feel comfortable doing this chore yourself, discuss the problem with your groomer. Shorter hair prevents the transference of bacteria and avoids trauma from scrapes and scratches.

Dogs love to hang their heads out of car windows, but this can result in eye injuries and serious infection from blowing debris. If you don't want to deprive your dog of this simple pleasure, I recommend a product called Doggles.

These protective goggles for dogs come in a range of colors and sizes for less than $20 / £12 per pair. The investment in protecting your dog's eyes is well worth it. All my pets have worn the Doggles without complaint.

Conjunctivitis is the most common eye infection seen in dogs. It presents with redness around the eyes and a green or yellow discharge. Antibiotics will treat the infection. The dreaded "cone of shame" collar then prevents more injury from scratching during healing.

Cataracts

Aging dogs often develop cataracts, which is a clouding of the lens of the eye leading to blurred vision. The lesion can vary in size and will be visible as a blue-gray area. In most cases, the vet will watch but not treat cataracts. The condition does not affect your pet's life in a severe way. Dogs adapt well to the senses they do have, so diminished vision is not as problematic as it would be for us.

Cherry Eye

The condition called "cherry eye" is an irritation of the third eyelid. It appears as a bright pink protrusion in the corner of the eye. Either injury or a bacterial infection causes cherry eye. It may occur in one or both eyes and requires surgery to give a permanent cure.

Glaucoma

With glaucoma, increased pressure prevents proper drainage of fluid. Glaucoma may develop on its own or as a complication of a shifted cataract. Dogs with glaucoma experience partial or total loss of vision within one year of diagnosis.

Symptoms include swelling, excessive tearing, redness and evident visual limitations. Suspected glaucoma requires immediate medical attention.

PRA or Progressive Retinal Atrophy

Progressive Retinal Atrophy (PRA), a degenerative hereditary disease, presents with a slow progression. The dog will go blind over time, but most adapt to what is happening to them. Early detection allows for better environmental adaptations.

Amy Lane of Fox Creek Farm has good news on PRA:

"Fortunately the DNA markers have been found for this disease (as well as Von Willebrand's disease), meaning with responsible testing and breeding they are completely avoidable now. A simple cheek swab sent to a lab will determine if a dog is clear, a carrier or affected by this disease. They are recessive genes, so both parents would have to be a carrier or one a carrier and one affected for offspring to be affected, which means they would go blind. Being a carrier is fine from a health standpoint. A carrier can safely be bred to a clear dog and no puppies will be affected. Some will be carriers."

If you suspect your Goldendoodle has poor peripheral vision or if the dog is tentative in low light, have your pet's eyes checked.

Hemorrhagic Gastroenteritis

Any dog can develop hemorrhagic gastroenteritis (HGE). The condition has a high mortality rate. Unfortunately, most dog owners have never heard of HGE. If a dog does not receive immediate treatment, the animal may well die.

Symptoms include:

* profuse vomiting
* depression
* bloody diarrhea with a foul odor
* severe low blood volume resulting in fatal shock within 24 hours

The exact cause of HGE is unknown, and it often occurs in otherwise healthy dogs. The average age of onset is 2-4 years. Approximately 15% of dogs that survive an attack will suffer a relapse. There is no definitive list of high-risk breeds. Those with a high incidence rate include:

* Miniature Poodles
* Miniature Schnauzers
* Yorkshire Terriers
* Dachshunds

The instant your dog vomits or passes blood, get your dog to the vet. Tests will rule out viral or bacterial infections, ulcers, parasites, cancer and poisoning. X-rays and an electrocardiogram are also primary diagnostic tools for HGE.

Hospitalization and aggressive treatment are necessary. The dog will likely need IV fluids and even a blood transfusion. Both steroids and antibiotics prevent infection. If the dog survives, the animal should eat a bland diet for a week or more, with only a gradual reintroduction of normal foods. In almost all cases, the dog will eat a special diet for life with the use of a probiotic.

The acute phases of HGE lasts 2-3 days. With quick and aggressive treatment, many dogs recover well. Delayed intervention for any reason means the outlook is not good.

Photo Credit: Laura Chaffin of Cimarron Frontier Doodles

Tail Docking or Cropping

Breeders use both Golden Retrievers and Poodles to create the Goldendoodle. Neither of those breeds has a naturally short tail. At some breeders, before the puppy reaches adulthood, the tail is "docked" or cut. This is a controversial practice in Goldendoodles and one that serious enthusiasts seek to end.

Most owners don't want the dogs to go through painful mutilation for no good reason. Often the procedure occurs long before puppies come up for adoption. Some breeders take puppies to the vet for the surgery under anesthesia. Others remove the tails within five days of birth.

The assumption is that puppies have underdeveloped nervous systems and don't feel intense pain. Breeders use one of two methods.

- A strong band on the tail cuts off circulation to the tip until it falls off from dry gangrene.

- A clamp on the tail controls bleeding for amputation of the remaining section with a scalpel or scissors.

Regardless of where the procedure occurs, the wound requires stitches.

If you are against docking a dog's tail, make this clear when you contact a breeder. If they know in advance, most will leave the tail intact, but you are then obligated to take the dog.

Docking is illegal in the United Kingdom and Australia. Efforts are underway in parts of the United States to ban the practice, but no laws currently exist.

Chapter 7 – Preparing for Older Age

It can be heartbreaking to watch your beloved pet grow older – he may develop health problems like arthritis, and he simply might not be as active as he once was.

Unfortunately, aging is a natural part of life that cannot be avoided. All you can do is learn how to provide for your Goldendoodle's needs as he ages so you can keep him with you for as long as possible.

Photo Credit: Bev and Arnie Eckert of Hilltop Pups

What to Expect

Aging is a natural part of life for both humans and dogs.

Sadly, dogs reach the end of their lives sooner than most humans do.

Once your Goldendoodle reaches the age of 10 years or so, he can be considered a "senior" dog.

At this point, you may need to start feeding him a dog food specially formulated for older dogs, and you may need to take some other precautions as well.

In order to properly care for your Goldendoodle as he ages, you might find it helpful to know what to expect. On this page, you will find a list of things you might notice as your Goldendoodle dog starts to get older:

• Your dog may be less active than he was in his youth – he will likely still enjoy walks, but he may not last as long as he once did, and he might take it at a slower pace.

• Your Goldendoodle's joints may start to give him trouble – check for signs of swelling and stiffness, and consult your veterinarian with any problems.

• Your dog may sleep more than he once did – this is a natural sign of aging, but it can also be a symptom of a health problem, so consult your vet if your dog's sleeping becomes excessive.

• Your dog may have a greater tendency to gain weight, so you will need to carefully monitor his diet to keep him from becoming obese in his old age.

• Your dog may have trouble walking or jumping, so keep an eye on your Goldendoodle if he has difficulty jumping, or if he starts dragging his back feet.

• Your dog's vision may no longer be as sharp as it once was, so your Goldendoodle may be predisposed to these problems.

• You may need to trim your Goldendoodle's nails more frequently if he doesn't spend as much time outside as he once did when he was younger.

• Your dog may be more sensitive to extreme heat and cold, so make sure he has a comfortable place to lie down both inside and outside.

• Your dog will develop gray hair around the face and muzzle – this may be less noticeable in Goldendoodles with a lighter coat.

While many of the signs mentioned above are natural side effects of aging, they can also be symptoms of serious health conditions.

If your dog develops any of these problems suddenly, consult your veterinarian immediately.

Caring for an Older Goldendoodle

When your Goldendoodle gets older, he may require different care than he did when he was younger.

The more you know about what to expect as your Goldendoodle ages, the better equipped you will be to provide him with the care he needs to remain healthy and mobile.

Here are some tips for caring for your Goldendoodle dog as he ages:

- Schedule routine annual visits with your veterinarian to make sure your Goldendoodle is in good condition.

- Consider switching to a dog food that is specially formulated for senior dogs – a food that is too high in calories may cause your dog to gain weight.

- Supplement your dog's diet with DHA and EPA fatty acids to help prevent joint stiffness and arthritis.

- Brush your Goldendoodle's teeth regularly to prevent periodontal diseases, which are fairly common in older dogs.

- Continue to exercise your dog on a regular basis – he may not be able to move as quickly, but you still need to keep him active to maintain joint and muscle health.

- Provide your Goldendoodle with soft bedding on which to sleep – the hard floor may aggravate his joints and worsen arthritis.

- Use ramps to get your dog into the car and onto the bed, if he is allowed, because he may no longer be able to jump.

- Consider putting down carpet or rugs on hard floors – slippery hardwood or tile flooring can be very problematic for arthritic dogs.

In addition to taking some of the precautions listed above in caring for your elderly Goldendoodle, you may want to familiarize yourself with some of the health conditions your dog is likely to develop in his old age.

Elderly dogs are also likely to exhibit certain changes in

behavior, including:

- confusion or disorientation
- increased irritability
- decreased responsiveness to commands
- increase in vocalization (barking, whining, etc.)
- heightened reaction to sound
- increased aggression or protectiveness
- changes in sleep habits
- increase in house soiling accidents

As he ages, these tendencies may increase – he may also become more protective of you around strangers.

As your Goldendoodle gets older, you may find that he responds to your commands even less frequently than he used to.

The most important thing you can do for your senior dog is to schedule regular visits with your veterinarian. You should also, however, keep an eye out for signs of disease as your dog ages.

The following are common signs of disease in elderly dogs:

- decreased appetite
- increased thirst and urination
- difficulty urinating/constipation
- blood in the urine
- difficulty breathing/coughing
- vomiting or diarrhea
- poor coat condition

If you notice your elderly Goldendoodle exhibiting any of these symptoms, you would be wise to seek veterinary care for your dog as soon as possible.

Euthanasia

The hardest decision any pet owner makes is helping a suffering animal to pass easily and humanely. I have been in this position, and even though I know my beloved companied died peacefully and with no pain, my own anguish was considerable. Thankfully, I was in the care of and accepting the advice and counsel of exceptional veterinary professionals.

This is the crucial component in the decision to euthanize an animal. For your own peace of mind, you must know that you have been given the best medical advice possible. My vet was not only knowledgeable and patient, but she was kind and forthright. I valued all of those qualities and hope you are as blessed as I was in the same situation.

But the bottom line is this: No one is in a position to judge you. No one. You must make the best decision that you can for your pet and for yourself. So long as you are acting from a position of love, respect and responsibility, whatever you do is "right."

Grieving a Lost Pet

Some humans have difficulty fully recognizing the terrible grief involved in losing a beloved canine friend.

There will be many who do not understand the close bond we humans can have with our dogs, which is often unlike any we have with our human counterparts.

Your friends may give you pitying looks and try to cheer you up, but if they have never experienced the loss of such a special connection themselves, they may also secretly think you are making too much fuss over "just a dog."

For some of us humans, the loss of a beloved dog is so painful that we decide never to share our lives with another, because the thought of going through the pain of such a loss is unbearable.

Expect to feel terribly sad, tearful and yes, depressed, because those who are close to their canine companions will feel their loss no less acutely than the loss of a human friend or life partner.

The grieving process can take some time to recover from, and some of us never totally recover.

After the loss of a family dog, first you need to take care of yourself by making certain that you remember to eat regular meals and get enough sleep, even though you will feel an almost eerie sense of loneliness.

Losing a beloved dog is a shock to the system that can also affect your concentration and your ability to find joy or be interested in participating in other activities that are a normal part of your daily life.

Other dogs, cats and pets in the home will also be grieving the loss of a companion and may display this by acting depressed, being off their food or showing little interest in play or games.

Therefore, you need to help guide your other pets through this grieving process by keeping them busy and interested, taking them for extra walks and finding ways to spend more time with them.

Wait Long Enough

Many people do not wait long enough before attempting to replace a lost pet and will immediately go to the local shelter and rescue a deserving dog. While this may help to distract you from your grieving process, this is not really fair to the new fur member of your family.

Bringing a new pet into a home that is depressed and grieving the loss of a long-time canine member may create behavioral problems for the new dog that will be faced with learning all about their new home, while also dealing with the unstable energy of the grieving family.

A better scenario would be to allow yourself the time to properly grieve by waiting a minimum of one month to allow yourself and your family to feel happier and more stable before deciding upon sharing your home with another dog.

Managing Health Care Costs

Thanks to advances in veterinary science, our pets now receive viable and effective treatments. The estimated annual cost for a medium-sized dog, including health care, is $650 / £387. (This does not include emergency care, advanced procedures or consultations with specialists.)

The growing interest in pet insurance to help defray these costs is understandable. You can buy a policy covering accidents, illness, and hereditary and chronic conditions for $25 / £16.25 per month. Benefit caps and deductibles vary by company. To get rate quotes, investigate the following companies in the United States and the UK:

United States

http://www.24PetWatch.com
http://www.ASPCAPetInsurance.com
http://www.EmbracePetInsurance.com
http://www.HealthyPawsPetInsurance.com
http://www.PetsBest.com
http://www.PetInsurance.com
http://www.trupanion.com/

United Kingdom

http://www.Animalfriends.org.uk
http://www.Healthy-pets.co.uk
http://www.Petplan.co.uk
http://www.Vetsmedicover.co.uk

Afterword

Now that you have more information and a greater understanding of the Goldendoodle cross, I hope you are in a position to decide if this is the right dog for you. The one "drawback" to adopting a mixed breed animal is the potential for inconsistency.

At first, Goldendoodles were crosses between Golden Retrievers and Standard Poodles. Now there are Goldendoodles of all sizes, and a whole "subset" derived from mixes with the European Golden Retriever.

Your best bet is to find a reputable breeder and to spend time with that person learning about how they breed their dogs and what qualities they are seeking to cultivate. Never adopt a dog unless you can visit the breeder and interact with the animals.

No adoption of a dog like a Goldendoodle should be a transaction based purely on cash in hand. Breeders know their dogs, and they know how to evaluate proper placement for their animals. When you work with a good breeder, you have an adoption partner and a source of information in the future if you have questions, concerns or problems.

Every Goldendoodle I have known has been a gentle, sweet devoted dog with an outstanding personality. Kids just love these dogs, and the dogs love them right back. Goldendoodles get along well with the pets and are accepting of strangers. They tend to be flexible dogs that more or less roll with the punches.

Goldendoodles are, however, active and enthusiastic pets. You will need to commit to at least a half an hour a day of activity with your dog. Goldendoodles are people dogs. They don't just want to be let out in the backyard. They want you out there as well, preferably with a ball in your hand!

If you have the time to commit to one of these dogs, you will have a devoted companion with a lifespan of as much as 16 years. Consider this commitment seriously, and if you decide to go ahead, prepare for your life to be changed by a lovable bundle of golden fur who, from the moment he sees you, will think you are the best thing EVER.

Photo Credit: Janet Wright of Okefeild Acres

Bonus Chapter 1 - Interview With April Cliber

I know you have been breeding Goldendoodles for some time, can you tell us for how long and how did it all start for you?

I am a wife, mom of two and professional puppy snuggler. I cannot get enough of these silly, fun-loving, fluffy companions we call Goldendoodles. Our home is in southeast Michigan.

When our kids were very young we were looking for a family dog. I preferred a standard Poodle and my husband requested a Lab. We compromised and got a new type of dog called a Labradoodle. Our wonderful doodle adventure started with Gracie, our Labradoodle. Gracie was everything we wanted and so much more! Her temperament was incredible and she became the ideal family member for us. As the children grew I wanted to work from home. My love of all animals, infatuation with doodles, photography interest and a background in sales were all factors in deciding to become a doodle breeder. I spent several months poring over books, consulting established breeders, gathering information from my veterinarian and carefully considering the time and commitment that would be required. I figured out exactly what type of breeder I wanted to be. I had a very clear vision of what my program would look like and customer service would be in the forefront. I wanted to raise puppies in our home focusing on socialization. I wanted to be everything I would expect in an excellent breeder. In 2006 we welcomed our first litter of Goldendoodles into the world. For a few years we bred both Labradoodles and Goldendoodles. In 2009 we decided to focus our program on Goldendoodles and move towards multigen litters. At 12 years old Gracie still remains an inspiration and valued family member.

You are one of the founding members of GANA, the Goldendoodle Association of North America. How did that start and what made you get involved?

While attending a breeder's conference in 2007, I was speaking with a breeder about the need to establish a Goldendoodle club and database registry. She introduced me to Amy Lane, another Goldendoodle breeder, who had similar thoughts. We discussed ideas and agreed to contact each other in the future. About a year later, I received a call from Amy. She was in contact with a company willing to create the software that would be needed to start a database. I was thrilled to get started and immediately agreed to jump on board. That year Amy and I, along with Teri Fann of Goldens-n-Doodles set up the framework which included by-laws, breeder policies and guidelines, code of ethics, a Goldendoodle generation grading scheme and a website. Since we are all in different states, the majority of work was done through hundreds of emails. We set up a board of breeder members to govern GANA. They are voted on annually by breeder members. Their voice is heard on all decisions. GANA members are required to submit health testing on all breeding dogs and agree to a strict code of ethics in order to remain within the organization.

What types of people are buying Goldendoodles and why?

The ideal person/family will have plenty of time to devote to their dog. There is a broad range of ages and demographics. The desire for an active, social dog in their lives is their motivation. Goldendoodles thrive when surrounded by people, love and consistency.

What type of health issues can a Goldendoodle have and how do you deal with preventing these?

Health issues that affect Goldendoodles are the same that affect their parent breeds, Golden Retrievers and Poodles. We health test each parent before breeding them and follow the GANA Blue Ribbon requirements which include:

Hip evaluation from OFA, OVC, PennHip or Dr. Wallace
Elbow evaluation from OFA, OVC or Dr. Wallace
Clear patella (hind leg knees) evaluation for Mini Goldendoodles and Poodles
Cardiac OFA clearance for Goldendoodles and Golden Retrievers
CERF eye exams
Prcd-PRA DNA testing for genetic eye disease
DNA testing for Von Willebrand's Disease

Health testing parent dogs and responsible breeding practices greatly decrease the chances of puppies suffering the above.

Is it possible to describe a fairly typical Goldendoodle?

The Goldendoodle is a loving, whimsical dog known for its exceptional intelligence and trainability. Goldendoodles are social, friendly and extremely intuitive. He thoroughly enjoys being with "his people" and will be sad if left alone for long periods of time. A typical Goldendoodle has a fluffy, stuffed animal like appearance and a silly personality. Their antics are sure to entertain. If left alone, a Goldendoodle can, and many times will get into mischief. It's important they be properly supervised and engaged with family activities.

Can you offer advice to people looking to buy?

Evaluate your lifestyle and make sure you are ready and willing to take on the commitment of a puppy. Decide which size and generation of Goldendoodle is right for you. Take your time choosing your breeder. Thoroughly read over websites and information. Ask questions and do your homework. You can learn a lot about a breeder when communicating with them. Are they passionate about what they do? Are they knowledgeable about their dogs and puppies? Are they open and eager to educate you? If possible, visit a breeder in person. Because of the risk of disease, many breeders limit visits or have designated times for visits. Don't be surprised when you are asked to take off your shoes and wash your hands. Never visit more than one breeder in a day. This is how germs and disease are spread. If you can't visit, ask for references, and follow up. Many breeders now have social media pages. Joining them will help you make connections with people who can give references.

A responsible Goldendoodle breeder will:

• Never promise a completely hypoallergenic dog. Although many Goldendoodles are low shedding and some don't shed at all, there are no guarantees.

• Do thorough health testing on all parent dogs, and will be willing to show you testing when asked.

• Offer at least a two year health warranty and never require the dog be returned to the breeder in order to honor the warranty.

www.Cliberdoodle.com

Are there things new owners do that perhaps frustrate you?

My biggest point of frustration is when people come to me for a "perfect" dog. There are exactly as many perfect dogs in the world as there are perfect people. All dogs are work, require a lot of time and energy and will develop bad habits if allowed. Puppies will be energetic, jump, nip and chew. They will have accidents in the house. Before deciding to get any puppy, please honestly evaluate your lifestyle to make sure you will have the time and dedication. Getting a Goldendoodle is typically a 12-15 year commitment. It isn't fair to the puppy if you are not ready and able to care for him for the duration of his life.

Are there any tips you would like to share with new owners?

I always stress the importance of pet insurance. Insurance is now very reasonably priced and well worth the peace of mind it will bring. Puppies are notorious for getting into things they shouldn't, especially during the first year. Some ingest objects such as socks and dish towels. One trip to the emergency vet can easily cost $1,000 or more. If surgery is required, $3,000 can be reached very quickly. Having insurance can make it possible to get the care a Goldendoodle needs during an illness or injury.

Start brushing your puppy as soon as they come home so they become accustomed to it. The coat of a Goldendoodle does require upkeep and maintenance. If you don't thoroughly brush at least three times a week, they will become matted. Make sure you are brushing all the way down to the skin and don't forget the armpits, behind the ears and the neck. A slicker brush works really well. Use a soft-bristled brush for young puppies and be gentle when you brush. It should be a pleasant experience for both you and your Goldendoodle. Begin professional grooming when your puppy is about 5-6 months old. Make sure to choose a groomer who has experience with grooming Goldendoodles and will be patient and kind. A Goldendoodle should be professionally groomed 3-6 times a year, depending on the coat.

Puppy-proof your house the same way you would for a baby. Keep all small items up on shelves or behind gated rooms. Legos, small dolls and toys should be played with in a room puppy is not allowed in. Teach kids to put all dirty clothes immediately in the hamper, especially socks. Start this before your puppy comes home so that it's already a habit. Keep all dish cloths and towels up high or in the cupboard. Do not hang them on the oven or refrigerator handle. Don't give a puppy a rope fleece or braided fleece toy. The knot can be swallowed whole resulting in a complete blockage that will require surgery.

You are getting a puppy to be a companion and family member. No doubt he will be work but he will be so worth it! Snuggle with your puppy, play fetch, take him with you for a quick trip to get coffee at the drive through, take him with you to pick up the kids from school. Play games, make up silly voices for your puppy, sing songs to him and enjoy his antics. Your puppy will change your life....for the better!

Thank you April for sharing your expertise with everyone.

April Cliber of Cliberdoodle
http://www.cliberdoodle.com/

Bonus Chapter 2 - Interview With Amy Lane

Amy thanks for doing this interview, can you tell us who you are and where you are based?

I am Amy Lane, one of the founding breeders of the Goldendoodle, the creator of the mini Goldendoodle, and the founding president of GANA (Goldendoodle Association of North America, Inc). I spent most of my life in Maryland which is where I was located when I began breeding dogs. I moved to Berkeley Springs, WV in 2005 to build a custom kennel and to expand my breeding business which my husband David is also involved in.

What inspired you to become a breeder and did you start with Goldendoodles?

I grew up riding and competing with horses. I dabbled in breeding horses for my own use as well as for my children's use. I began breeding Golden Retrievers in the 1990s more as a hobby than as a way to make a living. At that time, I was also helping a longtime friend market her Labradoodle puppies. She was the first to produce American Labradoodles in the USA and very few people had heard of a Labradoodle.

When a stray stud pony wandered onto my farm and kicked and killed my Golden Retriever stud dog, I had to make some quick decisions about the future of my breeding Golden Retrievers. Since I needed about 2 years to find, raise and health test a new Golden Retriever puppy to replace my stud, I decided to try breeding a Golden Retriever to a Poodle. When families came to pick up their reserved Labradoodle puppy, I showed them the litter of Golden Retriever/Poodle crosses and half of the families changed their mind and settled on the Golden Retriever/Poodle crosses instead of a Labradoodle. When I was asked what breed the puppies were, I wasn't sure what to say. I just blurted out "Goldendoodle" and the name stuck. For many years, customers couldn't help giggling when they stated they were calling about my Goldendoodle puppies.

How did things progress to the point of you becoming a co-founder of GANA - the Goldendoodle Association of North America?

I attended a conference 2007 in Orlando that was basically for Labradoodle breeders. It was geared towards educating breeders and I felt this was a great benefit to the breeders that belonged to the ALAA (Australian Labradoodle Association of America). I started talking to other Goldendoodle breeders that also attended and mentioned I would like to work towards creating a similar association for Goldendoodle breeders. I felt that as the Goldendoodle developed beyond the F1 (Golden Retriever crossed with a Poodle) that a registry database was necessary to avoid breeding related dogs as breeders were beginning to trade breeding stock to diversify their lines. As I was leaving the conference, April Cliber (whom I had never met before) approached me to say she would be happy to work on creating an organization when and if I decided to move forward with this idea. It took me several months of research and I then had a local attorney create the Articles of Incorporation and I obtained non-profit status from the IRS. I was in contact with the person that had created the registry database for the ALAA and worked out a price for the modifications we would need. I put up the initial $2500 down payment for the software. I then contacted April and asked if she was still interested in working on this venture with me. She was surprised I even remembered her offer. My response was that I would never forget someone that offered to help. :)

At about that same time, I had been communicating with a breeder in TN from which I was considering purchasing a breeding prospect. I was impressed with Teri Fann's background as a paralegal and her professional approach in how she fielded my questions. I asked her if she was interested in working on this new organization with April and myself. She agreed to join us and the three of us worked non-stop for perhaps the next year creating the structure of GANA (Goldendoodle Association of North America, Inc.). We created the Code of Ethics, the health testing requirements and the general membership rules.

I had a good friend, Lori Edmonds, who agreed to create our website and be our Registrar for the registry database. Lori continues to be our webmaster, but as GANA earned enough to pay off the software cost and to reimburse me for my original investment, we have since hired a Registrar, Anthea McCallister, who is the only paid person involved with GANA. We have had other breeder members serve on the GANA Board over the years, but I am the only original member that has held a board position since the inception of GANA.

What are the aims of GANA and how is it likely to develop in the future?

Each breed of dog has a kennel club that determines the direction of the breed's future based on the input from its members. GANA is the first kennel club developed for Goldendoodles. It is my hope that all breeders realize their voice is important. No one breeder can determine a breed standard. We have a great membership of quality breeders who have been sharing information about their different experiences throughout the development of their personal lines. They have been trading breeding stock and providing feedback to the other members. As new health testing becomes available, breeders can vote whether to require the new test or not. It is important as the breed standard is developed and set by the GANA membership, that the great qualities produced by other reputable breeders are recognized as important to the breed as well. It is in this ground floor stage of a new breed that breeders passionate about the development have input.

You are the first person to breed the mini Goldendoodle, can you tell us a bit more about what this is and why you did this?

I had many prospective customers who made a standard Goldendoodle comment that they loved the concept, the look and the temperament of the Goldendoodle, but that a smaller dog would fit their lifestyle better. I decided to find a quality mini Poodle stud to hire to create a litter as an experiment. I created a website to market these puppies and had them sold by the time they were born. The litter produced 10 puppies that arrived on 1/11/02 and I retained two to evaluate for possible future breeding. I placed one in a guardian home (Lucy) and I raised the other female (Pebbles).

Everyone that met these dogs just had to have one and the mini Goldendoodles' popularity soared. I then purchased a male mini Poodle puppy to continue creating more litters. It was this mini Poodle, Radar that I bred to Pebbles to create the first F1B mini litter. The first litter of F1 minis all lived to celebrate their 12th birthday. Eight of the ten have lived to thirteen years of age.

Photo Credit: PortraitsInTheSand.com

There are a number of variations within the Goldendoodle breed, perhaps you could explain which types you breed?

As with any new breed, there are levels of development. I started out producing the first cross of a Poodle and a Golden Retreiver called F1s. This generation provides offspring with a 50% chance of shedding coats. Each time I have developed a deeper generation, it has been with a goal in mind to improve upon something. In crossing an F1 Goldendoodle with a Poodle, the F1B generation is created. In my lines, this F1B generation maintains about a 90% non-shedding success rate. I now only produce multigens which are the product of crossing two Goldendoodles. The Goldendoodles used to create a multigen litter can have only one F1 parent as crossing two F1 Goldendoodles produces an F2 litter which is not considered to be a multigen. I have concentrated on the multigen Goldendoodle due to the higher non-shedding success rate. My personal lines tend to have a 98% non-shedding success rate making them the best generation for those that suffer from mild to moderate dog-related allergies.

The most popular dog in the USA is consistently the Labrador Retriever, why might people look at a Goldendoodle instead and can you see the Goldendoodle becoming one of America's most popular breeds of dog?

The Labrador Retriever has achieved the most popular dog status due to a predictable even keeled temperament and a no-maintenance coat. It is also a breed that is riddled with health issues due to the fact that over breeding and inbreeding are commonplace to keep up with the steady demand for more puppies. Even though the Goldendoodle is extremely popular, it would be detrimental for the breed to become the most popular dog in the USA. It would only lead to more puppy mills and backyard breeders trying to cash in on the higher demand for puppies. If all breeders followed GANA's requirements, we could all rest assured that the Goldendoodle would not suffer in a higher demand situation. However this is very unlikely.

What types of people are buying Goldendoodles?

In the beginning, the typical customer was a Golden Retriever lover that was allergic to shedding dogs. It was an option that allowed them to have a dog with the personality of the Golden Retriever, but without the allergy causing dander. As the popularity has soared, it is a middle to upper class family that purchases a health tested and guaranteed puppy as a quality bred Goldendoodle puppy has become quite pricey. The high price tag is dictated by the fact that many Poodle and Golden Retriever breeders will not sell their puppies to Goldendoodle breeders for use in breeding. It is also dictated by the fact that a breeder that has a high moral standard requiring a prospective breeding dog pass an entire regimen of health testing may raise many puppies only to learn that several will not be considered worthy of reproducing. This cost has to be absorbed somewhere to allow a breeder to continue producing only top quality puppies.

Can you offer advice to people looking to buy a Goldendoodle and how much should they be spending?

An educated buyer is appreciated by all quality breeders. A prospective customer needs to learn of the importance of health testing. They also should be concerned with the care given to their puppy in the first eight weeks of life. This is a critical time for a puppy and appropriate handling and care will play an important role in the rest of the puppy's life. A prospective customer should expect to pay a minimum of $2000 for a puppy coming from fully health-tested parents. A minimum of a two year genetic defect warranty should be expected and it should not require the return of the puppy to exercise the warranty.

A breeder should welcome you to visit, but they may not allow you to enter into the area where puppies are whelped and raised due to the risk of spreading germs. A good breeder will give you their attention to answer all your questions and to educate you on appropriate care in raising a puppy. A breeder that is not responsive to your questions before the sale will be even less responsive after you have taken your puppy home.

Do they attract a lot of interest and curiosity from the public?

I send out surveys to all my puppy families when their puppies are 6 and 12 months of age. The most common comment I receive on these surveys is that they cannot walk their puppy/dog down the road in peace. They have pedestrians and cars stopping them constantly asking for the breed name, about the personality, and where they can purchase one just like it. Even President Obama considered a Goldendoodle puppy before he was given a Portuguese Water Dog from Senator Kennedy. Hunter Biden, Joe Biden's son, has two Goldendoodles they purchased from me.

The Goldendoodle is not recognized by the American Kennel Club, is it a question or issue that is raised by many people?

A common question I receive is when do I expect the AKC to recognize the Goldendoodle? My response is always the same - hopefully never! GANA is unique in that the only dogs that can be registered as breeding dogs are those that have been health tested to GANA's standards. No inbreeding is allowed. The AKC does not promote nor require this as their only requirement is that the dog being registered was produced by two purebreds of the same breed. The AKC allows for registration of brothers and sisters bred together, fathers and daughters, mothers and sons. They allow dogs riddled with health issues to be registered and will even allow them to achieve championship status. GANA's mission statement says the "primary objective is to promote and guide the development of the Goldendoodle to achieve breed standards while maintaining optimum health."

What sort of challenges do you face in mating two different breeds?

The size difference when creating a litter out of and by two dogs of varying sizes requires many matings to be accomplished via artificial insemination. Two dogs that vary in size dramatically dictate the female be the larger of the two. A small female bred to a large male could prove disastrous as she may be too small to deliver large puppies. A small male many times cannot reach the larger female to perform a natural breeding. In these instances, artificial insemination is the only possibility. An experienced breeder can do this procedure without the assistance of a vet. When allowing a natural breeding, the male and the female know when the timing is exactly right for conception to occur and will typically only breed during this time. When performing an artificial insemination, it is up to the human to determine the time of ovulation so a pregnancy can be achieved. This requires progesterone testing which involves drawing a small amount of blood from the female to then run through a chemical test to determine if artificial breeding should occur or if it needs to wait. A canine reproductive specialist can take care of this entire process if a breeder doesn't have the skills or knowledge to accomplish this on their own.

What type of health issues can a Goldendoodle have and how do you deal with preventing these?

Goldendoodles can be affected by the same issues that Poodles or Golden Retrievers experience. The issues GANA has determined as being the most crucial for testing and avoiding are hip dysplasia, elbow dysplasia, numerous eye conditions, sub aortic stenosis, luxating patellas, Von Willebrand's Disease, and the Poodle and Golden Retriever mutations of Progressive Retinal Atrophy. Testing and certifying the hips, elbows, patellas, heart, and eyes prove the parent dog is not affected by any known conditions. The fact that the parent dog is normal gives a much better chance they will not produce puppies with issues of the heart, eyes, hips, elbows, or patellas. The testing done for Von Willebrand's Disease and PRA is via DNA. These genes are recessive meaning both parents have to be a carrier of the same issue for their puppies to inherit the issues and be affected by them. Testing a single parent in a breeding pair is enough to ensure none of the puppies will be affected by these issues.

What is the typical temperament of a Goldendoodle, so people know what to expect from their new pet?

Goldendoodles have a fun-loving temperament and many tend to exhibit a sense of humor. They are highly intelligent and have a great desire to please. They are an active dog that requires lots of human interaction to be happy. They are not the type of dog you leave in the fenced back yard to entertain themselves. They would much prefer to be touching a human and I tend to call them Velcro dogs. Many first time dog owners think a highly intelligent dog would be easier to raise and train because they are unsure of how to train a dog. The problem with this line of thinking is that many times the dog trains the humans instead of the other way around. Goldendoodles love to learn and do best when families new to raising a dog use the assistance of a trainer starting the day they bring home their new puppy.

Do you have any special feeding routines or diet?

I personally feed a dry food called Life's Abundance. It is a corn, wheat, dye, and preservative free food. I find it is best to feed puppies on a scheduled routine as it helps better predict bathroom needs which will ensure housebreaking is successful. Beyond the housebreaking stage, I allow my dogs to "graze" which means they can choose when they wish to eat. I find dogs maintained this way on dry food rarely have a weight issue.

What colors and sizes are most popular?

I personally receive more requests for the smaller sizes (minis and petites), but this may be because of my reputation for creating this size of Goldendoodle. I think there are more breeders producing standards as even inexperienced breeders can be successful in mating two larger dogs together. When a breeder needs to use artificial insemination to achieve a pregnancy, it decreases the number of breeders producing the smaller size Goldendoodles. It used to be that golden and blonde were the only colors available. Since Poodles come in multiple colors, other colors have been added to the Goldendoodle color spectrum. I find my most requested color currently is red.

As a breed expert, are there any 'essential' tips you would like to share with new owners?

Raising a puppy is similar to raising a child. The more effort and energy you provide in the formative stages, the more mannerly dog you will have to enjoy throughout its life. All puppies have the ability to learn and be an integral part of the family. The puppies that do not succeed or that have behavioral issues are always due to human error. It is very easy for the human to blame the breeder for the puppy's failure, but unless it is a physical deficiency causing the problem, it can always be traced back to conscious or unconscious conditioning by the humans.

Amy, thank you for taking the time to share your tips and knowledge of the Goldendoodle.

Amy Lane of Fox Creek Farm Goldendoodles
http://www.goldendoodles.net/

Glossary

Abdomen – The surface area of a dog's body lying between the chest and the hindquarters, also referred to as the belly.

Allergy – An abnormally sensitive reaction to substances including pollens, foods or microorganisms. May be present in humans or animals with similar symptoms including, but not limited to, sneezing, itching and skin rashes.

Anal glands – Glands located on either side of a dog's anus used to mark territory. May become blocked and require treatment by a veterinarian.

Arm – On a dog, the region between the shoulder and the elbow is referred to as the arm or the upper arm.

Artificial insemination – The process by which semen is artificially introduced into the reproductive tract of a female dog for the purposes of a planned pregnancy.

Back – That portion of a dog's body that extends from the withers (or shoulder) to the croup (approximately the area where the back flows into the tail.)

Backyard breeder – Any person engaged in the casual breeding of purebred dogs with no regard to genetic quality or consideration of the breed standard is referred to as a backyard breeder.

Bitch – The appropriate term for a female dog.

Breed – A line or race of dogs selected and cultivated by man from a common gene pool to achieve and maintain a characteristic appearance and function.

Breed standard – A written "picture" of a perfect specimen of a given breed in terms of appearance, movement and behavior as formulated by a parent organization, for example, the American Kennel Club or in Great Britain, The Kennel Club.

Brows – The contours of the frontal bone that form ridges above a dog's eyes.

Buttocks – The hips or rump of a dog.

Castrate – The process of removing a male dog's testicles.

Chest – That portion of a dog's trunk or body encased by the ribs.

Coat – The hair covering a dog. Most breeds have both an outer coat and an undercoat.

Come into season – The point at which a female dog becomes fertile for purposes of mating.

Congenital – Any quality, particularly an abnormality, present at birth.

Crate – Any portable container used to house a dog for transport or provided to a dog in the home as a "den."

Crossbred – Dogs are said to be crossbred when each of their parents is of a different breed.

Dam – A term for the female parent.

Dew claw – The dew claw is an extra claw on the inside of the leg. It is a rudimentary fifth toe.

Euthanize – The act of relieving the suffering of a terminally ill animal by inducing a humane death, typically with an overdose of anesthesia.

Groom – To make a dog's coat neat by brushing, combing or trimming.

Harness - A cloth or leather strap shaped to fit the shoulders and chest of a dog with a ring at the top for attaching a lead. An alternative to using a collar.

Haunch bones – Terminology for the hip bones of a dog.

Haw – The membrane inside the corner of a dog's eye known as the third eyelid.

Head - The cranium and muzzle of a dog.

Hip dysplasia – A condition in dogs due to a malformation of the hip resulting in painful and limited movement of varying degrees.

Hindquarters – The back portion of a dog's body including the pelvis, thighs, hocks and paws.

Hock – Bones on the hind leg of a dog that form the joint between the second thigh and the metatarsus. Known as the dog's true heel.

Inbreeding – When two dogs of the same breed that are closely related mate.

Kennel – A facility where dogs are housed for breeding or an enclosure where dogs are kept.

Lead – Any strap, cord or chain used to restrain or lead a dog. Typically attached to a collar or harness. Also called a leash.

Litter – The puppy or puppies from a single birth or "whelping."

Muzzle – That portion of a dog's head lying in front of the eyes and consisting of the nasal bone, nostrils and jaws.

Neuter - To castrate or spay a dog thus rendering them incapable of reproducing.

Pedigree - The written record of a pedigreed dog's genealogy. Should extend to three or more generations.

Puppy – Any dog of less than 12 months of age.

Puppy mill – An establishment that exists for the purpose of breeding as many puppies for sale as possible with no consideration of potential genetic defects.

Separation anxiety – The anxiety and stress suffered by a dog left alone for any period of time.

Sire – The accepted term for the male parent.

Spay – The surgery to remove a female dog's ovaries to prevent conception.

Whelping – Term for the act of giving birth to puppies.

Withers – The highest point of a dog's shoulders.

Index